"Pedagogical gold! Barry Jones has produced an illuminating and moving guide to theological interpretation, framed as a sustained exploration of Psalm 90, and drawing on categories developed by theologian Gabriel Fackre. Jones hoped to show his students how to appreciate both traditional and critical approaches to Scripture while also moving beyond them. He has succeeded admirably, and now I can thankfully use his book with my own students."

—STEPHEN B. CHAPMAN
Associate Professor of Old Testament
Duke Divinity School

"More than a recent trend in biblical and theological scholarship, theological interpretation of Scripture is nothing less than the church's engagement with the Bible as Christian Scripture and not merely as a collection of ancient Mediterranean religious texts. But how to practice this approach to reading Scripture is a daunting challenge for ministers trained in historical-critical interpretive methodologies (as well they should be). Barry Jones provides theological students and theologically educated ministers with a helpful apprenticeship in this art—not a theoretical introduction, but an invitation to join him in the actual practice of reading a particular biblical text theologically."

—STEVEN R. HARMON
Associate Professor of Historical Theology
Gardner-Webb University School of Divinity

Smyth & Helwys Publishing, Inc.
6316 Peake Road
Macon, Georgia 31210-3960
1-800-747-3016
©2019 by Barry A. Jones
All rights reserved.

Library of Congress Cataloging-in-Publication Data

Names: Jones, Barry A. (Barry Alan), 1962- author.
Title: Gaining a heart of wisdom : a model for theological interpretation of
   Scripture / by Barry A. Jones.
Description: Macon, GA : Smyth & Helwys Publishing, 2019. | Includes
   bibliographical references.
Identifiers: LCCN 2018058926 | ISBN 9781641730938 (pbk. : alk. paper)
Subjects: LCSH: Bible--Hermeneutics. | Bible--Theology. | Wisdom--Religious
   aspects.
Classification: LCC BS476 .J665 2019 | DDC 220.601--dc23
LC record available at https://lccn.loc.gov/2018058926

BARRY A. JONES

Gaining *a* Heart *of* Wisdom

A MODEL FOR THEOLOGICAL INTERPRETATION OF SCRIPTURE

Also by Barry A. Jones

The Formation of the Book of the Twelve: A Study in Text and Canon

To Beth, Claire, and Nate
For your love, encouragement, and support

Acknowledgments

This book grew out of my teaching experience with doctor of ministry degree students at Campbell University Divinity School. Most people have the luxury of preferring either a devotional or an academic approach to reading the Bible, but the ministers in my seminars, like most ministers, are expected to move between these two worlds at a moment's notice. In my seminar titled "Classical Resources for Contemporary Ministry," these ministry colleagues have taught me a great deal about using all of the resources of the academy and the church in interpreting the Bible. This book is inspired by the faithfulness of the many ministers and pastors I know who study hard to "rightly divid[e] the word of truth" (2 Tim 2:15 KJV).

I am grateful to the administration of Campbell University for granting me a sabbatical in spring 2017 to conduct the research and much of the writing of this book. I am also grateful to my colleagues on the faculty of the Divinity School who helped in many ways, especially with covering my teaching responsibilities during the sabbatical. The book is dedicated to my family, whose support and encouragement made the completion of this project possible and who fill everything I do with meaning and joy.

PSALM 90

A Prayer of Moses, the man of God.

[1] Lord, you have been our dwelling place
    in all generations.
[2] Before the mountains were brought forth,
      or ever you had formed the earth and the world,
      from everlasting to everlasting you are God.
[3] You turn us back to dust,
    and say, "Turn back, you mortals."
[4] For a thousand years in your sight
    are like yesterday when it is past,
    or like a watch in the night.
[5] You sweep them away; they are like a dream,
    like grass that is renewed in the morning;
[6] in the morning it flourishes and is renewed;
    in the evening it fades and withers.
[7] For we are consumed by your anger;
    by your wrath we are overwhelmed.
[8] You have set our iniquities before you,
    our secret sins in the light of your countenance.
[9] For all our days pass away under your wrath;
    our years come to an end like a sigh.
[10] The days of our life are seventy years,
    or perhaps eighty, if we are strong;
  even then their span is only toil and trouble;
    they are soon gone, and we fly away.
[11] Who considers the power of your anger?
    Your wrath is as great as the fear that is due you.
[12] So teach us to count our days
    that we may gain a wise heart.
[13] Turn, O LORD! How long?
    Have compassion on your servants!
[14] Satisfy us in the morning with your steadfast love,
    so that we may rejoice and be glad all our days.
[15] Make us glad as many days as you have afflicted us,
    and as many years as we have seen evil.
[16] Let your work be manifest to your servants,
    and your glorious power to their children.
[17] Let the favor of the Lord our God be upon us,
    and prosper for us the work of our hands—
    O prosper the work of our hands!

Contents

Chapter 1

To Gain a Wise Heart:
A Prayer and a Quest

"So teach us to count our days that we may gain a wise heart." —Psalm 90:12

For much of my adult life, I have longed to achieve the goal voiced in this prayer in v. 12 of Psalm 90. "To count our days" means to count each day and to make each day count. It is a prayer to learn how to live out the limited time that I have in the wisest and most effective way possible. How can I make maximum use of the finite number of days I have to live? This is not a morbid question but a realistic one. Isaac Watts's famous paraphrase of Psalm 90 states the matter this way: "Time, like an ever-rolling stream, Bears all its sons away."[1] To navigate successfully the ever-flowing stream of time, minute by minute, hour by hour, and day by day, has long been a personal quest.

Though the goal of making each day count toward a wise and purposeful life is an inspiring one, it is also a goal that has remained beyond my reach. I could probably count on one hand the number of days I have used to maximum effect. I have sincere ambitions and have often devised carefully crafted plans for making each day count. Often, however, the unique pattern of my body's circadian rhythm has conspired to defeat me before I even get out of bed in the morning. If I do manage to rise on schedule and begin to focus on the well-planned agenda I outlined the night before, my easily distracted mind often goes off track, chasing a bread-crumb trail of random thoughts so that untold minutes evaporate before I even know it.

Some days, outside events interrupt my plans before my internal distractions do. However, I am able to string together enough accomplishments to want to try again the next day, sometimes with progress and sometimes feeling like Bill Murray's character in the movie *Groundhog Day*, waking up on February 2 to begin the same struggle again.

I have friends whose time in military service transformed their habits and mindset into a rigorous and disciplined use of seemingly every minute. If I were immersed in such a strictly ordered communal life, I am sure that I would internalize more of the habits that lead to well-ordered days. That has not been my story, however. I'm on my own in learning to count my days and make my days count without a military system to guide me. I have other friends who have spent long retreats in monasteries that pattern their days according to spiritual disciplines for marking time that have been established for centuries. This pattern of life is more rhythmic and peaceful than the one afforded by military discipline, but it is highly disciplined nevertheless. Monastic communities patterned after the Rule of St. Benedict establish an ordered life of worship and structure work around daily hours of corporate and private prayer. It is an appealing way of life, but, as observers such as Kathleen Norris have noted, it is not without its own challenges and tensions.[2] As admirable as such a life seems to be, like the great majority of people, I have not and likely will not join a monastic community.

In my quest to come to some peace about the way I manage time, I have done what other academics typically do: I've read books about it. Years ago, when I wanted to take up running, I started by collecting a small personal library about running. Following this same procedure, I have read all of the best-selling time-management books with titles like *The Seven Habits of Getting Things Done* and *Stop Procrastinating Yesterday*. I have purchased the most highly recommended organizational tools and daily planners, and even downloaded highly rated apps for scheduling and allocating my days in the hope of "filling the unforgiving minute with sixty seconds of distance run."[3] Although I have learned some helpful techniques and have acquired some better habits, all of these efforts have only served to confirm the words of Psalm 90:12. Successfully counting my days is not a matter of information, technique, or technology. It is a matter of wisdom.

Psalm 90 expresses the goal of successfully navigating the flow of time in a unique way. The result of learning to make each day count is to gain a *wise heart*. The uniqueness of this expression is partly the result of ancient physiology. Modern people speak of the heart as the seat of emotions. We value having a loving or tender heart. We describe knowledge, skill, and wisdom as faculties of the mind. In ancient Hebrew, the word "heart" most often described the inner life as opposed to the outer appearance. First Samuel 16:7 is a helpful example: "[Mortals] look on the outward appearance, but the LORD looks on the heart." Biblical Hebrew often uses the word "heart" to describe the range of internal experiences that include a person's thinking, will, emotions, attitudes, and even character. The heart is the inner sense of self that directs a person's total life. *Wisdom* in biblical language often means technical or administrative skill, but it also describes a kind of life that reflects the highest spiritual and ethical ideals, which are in turn reflections of God's own character. Mastering the journey through time requires more than knowledge, intellectual reasoning, or technical skill. It involves the moral knowledge to know what is right and good, the inner strength of will to choose it, and the personal determination to do it. Gaining a wise heart combines the personal dimensions of will, emotion, choice, and purpose with both the intellectual skills of knowledge and discernment and the practical skills of habit and action. Learning to make my days count so that I might gain a wise heart is ultimately a spiritual quest.

The most promising avenue for my quest to gain a wise heart lies down the path of personal vocation. I am a biblical scholar. The prayer of Psalm 90:12, "Teach us to count our days that we may gain a wise heart," is an opportunity to explore the depths of a biblical text for what it can teach me and others about making each day count in the quest for a life that is blessed by divine wisdom. This book describes what I have learned from exploring biblical texts as a student and from guiding others along these paths as a teacher. In addition to exploring the insight of Psalm 90 into living wisely, this book also addresses the larger issue of how to study and learn from biblical texts like Psalm 90 in ways that combine the best of both religious and academic resources for biblical study. This book presents a model for how interpreters of Scripture—ministers, theological students, and Christian disciples—can search the Scripture not only for the information it contains but also for the way it forms us as people in relation to God.

Psalm 90 appeals to me in the way that it names an ongoing struggle and a personal goal—to make the most of each day in order to learn to live wisely and well. The Bible itself is a treasury of texts that appeals to individuals and communities for myriad reasons. There are so many fascinating and inspiring texts within the Bible that interested readers often hardly know where to begin. The ways in which readers seek to understand and apply the content of biblical texts to their lives are also many and various. The Bible is read in certain ways in religious communities through Bible study groups and services of worship. The Bible is read in different ways altogether in academic settings, university courses, and the published works of professional biblical scholars. Popular culture reads, appropriates, and represents biblical texts in other ways that are often radically different from what one hears in either church or school. And each individual has his or own idiosyncratic way of making sense of biblical literature. When trying to understand the message of a biblical text and determine its importance for how people live their lives, what approaches to reading and interpretation should a person follow? One of the goals of this book is to demonstrate a model for reading biblical passages like Psalm 90 that gives primary attention to the Bible's role as sacred Scripture—as a text treasured and transmitted from generation to generation as a source of divine guidance and a vehicle for communion with God.

In this book, I describe a model of theological interpretation of the Bible that brings together different approaches to reading it in a way that is appropriate to the nature of the text as Scripture while also making use of the best resources that have been developed in the long history of biblical study. In the context of the theological interpretation of Scripture, the goal of gaining a wise heart takes on yet another layer of meaning. Wisdom includes making full use of the skills of critical interpretation of the Bible and, at the same time, integrating this knowledge into a life of spiritual integrity and unity that is symbolized by the biblical metaphor of the heart. A wise heart is one that can bring the best of critical study and spiritual devotion together in service to God and others.

At this point, it is important to address questions raised by the focus of this book: Isn't the study of a single text like Psalm 90 too narrow of a focus? Is the content of a single psalm enough to demonstrate the effectiveness of a model of theological interpretation? These are natural and important questions. With regard to Psalm 90, I will show that it is a profound text that probes deep questions of biblical faith. As a work of biblical poetry, it is an excellent example of poetry's ability to express a maximum of meaning in a minimum of words. The literary artistry and spiritual depth of Psalm 90 have brought comparison to the philosophical meditations of the book of Ecclesiastes and to the literary skill of the renowned Jewish sage Jesus Ben Sira, author of the deuterocanonical book of Ecclesiasticus. Within its seventeen verses, Psalm 90 addresses the themes of creation, time and eternity, divinity and humanity, justice, mercy, theodicy, wisdom, the fear of God, the nature of covenant, and the divine qualities of compassion, faithfulness, and grace.

With regard to the question of whether a focus on a single text is sufficient to demonstrate a model of theological interpretation effectively, recent writing about the theological interpretation of Scripture has argued for less theoretical discussion of hermeneutics and more concrete examples of interpretation of specific texts. For example, R. W. L. Moberly's 2013 book *Old Testament Theology: Reading the Hebrew Bible as Christian Scripture* takes the form of exegetical essays on specific biblical texts, arguing that what is needed is not more discussion about theological exegesis but rather more exegesis.[4] In addition to a stated need for concrete examples of theological interpretation of Scripture, the model of interpretation I am proposing has the goal of integrating the results of multiple theological disciplines such as Old Testament and New Testament studies, church history, systematic theology, and practical theology, disciplines that are often kept separate from each other by the tendency toward specialization in academic research. A study that takes into account the interpretation and influence of Psalm 90 within the literature and practice of these several fields can hardly be described as too narrow.

In order to show the need for a model of theological interpretation of Scripture, I will introduce the main outline and content of Psalm 90, setting the prayer for a wise heart in the context of the psalm as a whole. I will then describe the two major approaches that people have used in the past to gain greater understanding of biblical texts like Psalm 90. These two approaches are called *religious reading* and *critical reading*. I will discuss two examples of religious and critical readings of Psalm 90 in order to demonstrate the respective strengths and limitations of each approach. A comparison of the two primary ways of approaching the Bible will show why a third way of reading Psalm 90 and texts like it is needed, one that combines the strengths of religious and critical approaches while compensating for their individual weaknesses.

THE STRUGGLE TO COPE WITH TIME: AN INTRODUCTION TO PSALM 90

The prayer, "So teach us to count our days that we may gain a wise heart," serves as the turning point in the larger prayer of Psalm 90. The human experience of time is a major theme of the psalm as a whole. The first line of the psalm bears the title "The Prayer of Moses, the Man of God." It is the only writing in the book of Psalms attributed to the greatest leader of

ancient Israel and the fountainhead of Jewish faith. As a prayer from start
to finish, the psalm addresses God directly throughout its seventeen verses.
It sparkles with the captivating imagery and emotional energy that charac-
terize the Psalms as a whole while its unique content takes the reader on a
journey from praise to plea to petition.

Psalm 90 is a prayer almost entirely about time. The opening verse
praises God as the eternal dwelling place of God's people. St. Augustine
expressed the main thought of this verse in the opening book of his *Confessions*. There he asked how he could call God to come to him in prayer since
there was neither a place in Creation that could contain God nor a place
within himself where God was not already present. "Where do I call thee
to, when I am already in thee?" Augustine asked. "Or from whence would
thou come unto me? Where beyond heaven and earth, could I go that there
my God might come to me—he who hath said, 'I fill heaven and earth?'"[5]
Psalm 90 praises God as a sanctuary both in space and in time: "Before the
mountains were brought forth, or ever you formed the earth and the world,
from everlasting to everlasting, you are God" (v. 2). Isaac Watts captured
the eternal dimension of the opening doxology in his hymnic paraphrase:
"O God, our help in ages past/ our hope for years to come; / our shelter
from the stormy blast / and our eternal home." The praying community in
Psalm 90 locates itself within the boundary of God's eternal horizon.

Beyond the opening lines of praise in vv. 1-2, vv. 3-6 compare the
boundless dimensions of God's eternal nature with the challenges that arise
from the human experience of finitude. Echoing God's punishment of the
first humans in Genesis, the psalm complains that God has set a limit to
human life that divides humanity from God. Even a thousand years of
human history are in God's eyes like a single day that has already passed.
When compared to God's eternal nature, a millennium in human experience flourishes and fades like the desert grass that springs up with the
morning dew and withers in the noonday sun. Given these differing time
perspectives, God's eternal horizon for carrying out the work of redemption
may easily exceed the limits that a time-bound community has to witness
God's work firsthand. While God has all the time in the world, people do
not. This is not a problem for God, but it is for us.

Psalm 90's description of limited human time in relation to God's
unlimited perspective is similar to a concept from astronomy known as
the Copernican Principle. Prior to the work of Nicolaus Copernicus, the
dominant model of the universe held that the earth was at the center of a
perfectly circular system and that all observable heavenly bodies orbited

around it. Copernicus observed that this was not so. The Copernican Principle, derived from his discovery, states in its simplest form that the earth and its inhabitants do not occupy a special point of observation in the universe. Astrophysicist Richard Gott extended the use of the Copernican Principle to describe our place in time.[6] Gott paraphrased the Copernican Principle in relation to his own lifetime to mean "I'm not special." The point in time from which we observe history is not a privileged point in the sweep of time. Psalm 90 makes a similar observation. God's designs for the unfolding of human time are known only to God. The praying community of Psalm 90 cannot assume that their limited life span occupies a special place within the span of God's activity throughout history. Like a life raft adrift on a seemingly boundless ocean, time-bound mortals live without a shoreline in sight.

Although the idea of our exceedingly brief life in relation to God's eternal horizon is discouraging, vv. 7-11 point out that the actual situation is even worse than it appears. The problem of God's limitless horizon and humanity's brief life span is compounded by another factor that the psalmist calls "the wrath of God." The concept of God's wrath is an awkward and uncomfortable topic for many modern religious people. The Christian understanding of God as one whose love and mercy are revealed in the sacrificial death and victorious resurrection of Jesus creates tension with the idea of a God who acts on the basis of hostile emotions to punish and to harm. While there is much to be explored about the meaning of the language of divine wrath in the Bible, for now it is enough to say that the Old Testament uses the figurative language of the wrath of God very broadly to describe a wide range of negative experiences, including disasters, hardship, struggle, pain, and suffering.

Psalm 90:7-11 describes little of the specific circumstances that the community experiences as God's wrath. The primary problem with God's wrath addressed in these verses is its duration. The community's prolonged struggles threaten to overwhelm the maximum time frame, seventy or eighty years, that an ordinary person can normally expect to live. The general difficulty of managing the unceasing flow of time is compounded by a vague and prolonged experience of affliction. "All our days pass away under your wrath" (Ps 90:9).

It is in this context of feeling lost in the vastness of time and forgotten in the lingering silence of God that Psalm 90 turns from complaint to petition: "So teach us to count our days so that we may gain a wise heart." Verse 12 asks for help to cross an unmarked ocean of time under a sky of bronze through the divine gift of wisdom. Wisdom comes from learning from God how to count one's passing days.

The petition for divinely given wisdom serves as a turning point in the psalm. It unleashes a series of urgent requests, beginning with the plaintive lament, "Turn, O LORD! How long?" This echoes a prayer of Moses when he prayed that God would turn and relent from wrath in the wake of the Israelites' idolatry in the wilderness when they created and worshiped a golden calf (Exod 32:11-12). In the spirit of Moses' prayer, Psalm 90 urges God to turn, have compassion, and restore favor and mercy to a people living under wrath (v. 13). The psalmist asks for times of joy equal to the days and years of affliction. The psalm seeks some sense of proportion in time between suffering and joy (vv. 14-15). It also voices a hope that the favor of the Lord would be revealed to present and future generations as they had been revealed to generations past (v. 16). The psalm ends with a plea that the deeds of the very fragile and fleeting creatures who pray this prayer might somehow endure for future generations in God's sight. The final words of the psalm seek God's favor for ages to come in ways that reaffirm its earlier praise of God's help in ages past.

Psalm 90 is a profound prayer. It seeks a way to live wisely in time while holding together the extremes of God and humanity, mortality and eternity, suffering and joy, judgment and grace, despair and hope. It does so in conversation with major biblical themes of creation, redemption, covenant, and wisdom, all under the name of Israel's most important leader. Yet, to this point, I have described only the major landmarks of the text. How can a person come to know and appreciate all of the features of the world that Psalm 90 reveals in order to learn more fully about how to make each day count toward gaining a heart of wisdom?

TWO APPROACHES TO EXPLORING DEEPER MEANING IN PSALM 90

Of the various ways in which people have attempted to understand Psalm 90 and other Scripture like it, two major approaches have dominated all others. These two ways of interpreting Scripture are known as religious reading and critical reading.[7] Anyone who has attended a worship service or Bible study and has also taken a Bible course in a college or seminary is familiar with the primary orientation of each approach and with the differences between them. Each has strengths and weaknesses in discovering and making available scriptural meaning. Each continues to be practiced within its respective settings. I want to describe both ways of reading the Bible through the use of prominent examples in order to demonstrate the need for a third way of reading Scripture that weaves together the major strengths of religious reading and critical reading. **This third way, known as the theological interpretation of Scripture, has been emerging within the field of academic biblical studies over the past two decades. Psalm 90 will serve as a concrete example of a particular model of theological interpretation.**

Religious reading is a broad category that includes specific traditions of spiritual reading handed down in Catholic, Orthodox, and Protestant churches, as well as general features of religious interpretation that can be observed in scriptural religions in many times and places. Religious reading is performed by devotees of a religious tradition as a central form of their religious practice. The religious reader assumes a posture of submission to God and to the teachings of the sacred text through acquired skills of reading aimed at internalizing the words, images, and ideas of the text in a way that forms and transforms the identity and behavior of the reader from within.

Religion scholar Paul Griffiths studied the nature of religious reading by comparing the practices of scripture reading in Indian Buddhism and ancient African Christianity. He concluded from his comparative analysis that the reflective and transformational exercise of reading sacred texts is an essential practice of many religious traditions. He identified two key elements of religious reading. The first is an understanding of the religious work "as a stable and vastly rich resource, one that yields meaning, suggestions for action, matter for aesthetic wonder, and much else." The second key element is that religious readers are understood to be "intrinsically capable of reading and morally required to read."[8] All that is necessary for religious readers to receive inspiration and guidance from their sacred texts is already present in the texts themselves and in the readers themselves. One of the most important strategies of reading that Griffiths described is a process of internalization in which the reader memorizes and internalizes the text to such a degree that it has a formative influence on his or her thought, speech, and action. When religious texts are committed to memory and subjected to repeated reflection, the original literary settings and boundaries of the texts fade away and the words of the entire scriptural canon become woven together within the mind of the reader into a seamless tapestry of words, ideas, and images.[9]

Religious reading is an essential part of many religious traditions, including Christianity. It has been the primary mode of reading the Bible throughout Christian history and has been practiced continually in Christian traditions until the current day. Since the Enlightenment and the advent of the modern university, however, another form of reading has challenged and largely supplanted religious reading in some communities as the primary way of studying and appropriating the biblical text. Critical reading of the Bible developed out of the Renaissance and Reformation periods in Europe and took hold in European universities under the influence of the study of classical literature and the emerging methods of textual criticism, philology, literary-historical analysis, and comparative literature. As the religious conflicts arising out of the Reformation and Counter-Reformation fragmented European Christendom, critical study of the Bible in European universities sought to recover an original historical meaning of the text that could serve as common ground to unite a religiously divided Europe on cultural and intellectual rather than religious foundations.[10] In the late nineteenth and twentieth centuries, critical reading became the dominant method of studying the Bible in academic research, teaching, and publishing. The goal of critical study was to establish the meaning of the text on historical and linguistic grounds apart from the influence of religious and confessional commitments and established church doctrines.

It is important to note that religious and critical readings of the Bible are not mutually exclusive. Practitioners of each approach often share methods and characteristics in common. Religious readings often display impressive erudition and thorough immersion in the linguistic, textual, and literary details of the biblical text. Critical scholars often communicate the results of their studies to religious communities for religious purposes and are often members and even leaders of such communities themselves. The two approaches nevertheless represent two distinct types of reading, mostly as a result of their differing goals and particular institutional contexts.

Religious reading serves the goals of religious communities and devotees by making available intellectual, moral, and spiritual resources that are present or latent within sacred texts. The many methods of devotional study use the text as a window or a lens for understanding God, the world, and humanity, and the essential relationships among them. Such study takes place primarily in congregations or church-related institutions and is performed in continuity with a living tradition of interpretation that has been nurtured for centuries.

Critical study, by contrast, takes place primarily in educational settings and in the professional scholarly societies that support them. The goals of critical study are supportive of the generally secular goals of the modern university—to discover, preserve, apply, and hand down knowledge of the human and physical worlds. This knowledge uses the standards and criteria of reason necessary to minimize conflicting views and to adjudicate disputes. Assuming that personal commitments skew the results of critical study, such commitments, including religious ones, are either set aside or consciously devalued as part of the process of study. The aim is to secure knowledge that anyone could agree to, regardless of religious identity or cultural background. Most critical study of the Bible has focused on describing the historical development of the text and the most likely meaning of the text at its earliest identifiable point of origin.

RELIGIOUS AND CRITICAL READINGS OF PSALM 90: TWO EXAMPLES

The differences between religious study and critical study can be clarified by considering concrete examples of each approach as applied to Psalm 90. A classic example of a religious reading of Psalm 90 can be found in Matthew Henry's *Exposition on the Old and New Testament*, originally published between 1706 and 1710.[11] Henry's was the first English commentary on the entire Bible written for the common reader and has been continuously in print since its initial publication.[12] It needs to be said that Henry's commentary has been the bane of biblical studies professors for generations, not because it is of poor quality, but because it has long been in the public domain in both print and in electronic format and is perhaps the most widely available commentary on the whole Bible in the English language. As a result, almost any student studying almost any passage in the Bible has access to this commentary published before the critical study of the Bible was widely practiced and long before revolutionary discoveries were made in the mid- to late nineteenth century in the archaeology, literature, and languages of the ancient Near East. Students can access Henry's outlines, summaries, and pastoral applications of scriptural texts without having to give a thought to modern scholarship or to the historical evidence that biblical scholars prize most highly. In addition, Henry's summaries are so concise and his style is so compelling that students who use his work often conclude that their own thoughts on the text are rendered unnecessary in light of his potent summations.

Henry's commentary is a powerful representative of religious reading of Scripture. Henry received his primary education at home from his Oxford-trained father, a nonconforming pastor who was expelled from the Church of England after refusing to take the Oath of Uniformity following the restoration of the monarchy in 1660. The younger Henry pastored nonconforming churches in Chester and Hackney from 1687 until his death in 1714. The commentary grew out of his regular ministry of Bible teaching and preaching in his own church and in many other churches to which he was frequently invited as a visiting minister.[13] Henry's comments on Psalm 90 demonstrate the religious appeal of his work.

For Henry, the primary guide to understanding Psalm 90 was the title, "the prayer of Moses." He took this as both a title and a statement of authorship. Since the prayer comes from Moses, the logical question is, at what point in the life of Moses would such a prayer arise? Henry identified the events described in Numbers 14 as the most likely occasion. The Israel-ites had received the reports of the twelve spies who had gone in to spy out the promised land. They rejected the positive report of Caleb and Joshua and reacted to the fearful report of the spies who described the threat of the military strength of the land's inhabitants. As punishment for their lack of faith, the LORD sentenced those twenty years of age and older to live out the rest of their natural lives in the wilderness, never to enter the promised land. According to Henry, Moses composed Psalm 90 as a prayer for this condemned generation to be used for daily meditation and repentance. The circumstances of the prayer make it "applicable to the frailty of human life in general, and . . . we may easily apply it to the years of our passage through the wilderness of this world . . . ."[14]

Henry divided the psalm into four sections. Verses 1-2 describe the eternal care of God as a source of comfort in the wilderness setting of the Israelites and the daily trials of Christian readers. Verses 3-6 describe human frailty and urge humility. Many commentators interpret the phrase "you turn us back to dust" in v. 3 as a reference to Genesis 3:19 ("You are dust, and to dust you shall return"). In this view, human mortality is a universal punishment for sin and a lingering effect of the so-called fall. Henry, however, interpreted the statement in v. 3 as a description of divine punishment that is intended to lead to repentance: "You turn us back to dust (through punitive hardship), and say, 'Turn back (i.e., repent), you mortals.'" This interpretation is probably based on the fact that the Hebrew word for dust in v. 3 is different from the Hebrew word for dust in Genesis 3:19. Two other ancient scholars sensitive to the nuances of the Hebrew language, Jerome in the patristic era and the medieval Jewish exegete Rashi, offered the same interpretation of v. 3.[15]

Henry labeled vv. 7-11 as a confession of God's righteous judgment intended to cultivate a spirit of appropriate submission. As the teacher of

Israel, Moses instructed the Israelites to see their suffering as the righteous sentence of a just God and to respect the wrath of God as a corrective measure against human opposition to God's good plans. Verses 12-17 contain prayers for God's mercy intended to restore a sense of commitment to God's will. The wisdom sought in v. 12 is wisdom to lead a godly life. The prayer for mercy is a reminder that the generation of the exodus was spared immediate destruction as recorded in Numbers 14 in response to Moses' intercession. The prayer in v. 16 for God's work to be revealed to God's servants and their children teaches readers to pray with faith in the future success of God's work, remembering that though the exodus generation lived under judgment, their children did indeed receive the promised land.

The image Griffiths uses of religious texts—as an ocean or a mine that yields its riches to readers who make the effort to plumb the depths—describes well the process Henry used to interpret Psalm 90. By placing it in the narrative context of a tragic event in the story of Israel's wilderness journey, he added background, tone, and emotion to the lines of the prayer. The recontextualization of the prayer within the exodus narrative also gave it a greater degree of coherence. On a general level, the prayer "makes sense" in that setting. Although his comments on Psalm 90 were brief, as befitting a commentary on the whole Bible, they were nevertheless full of direct instruction and application. The religious aims of the comments did not come, however, at the expense of erudition. As noted above, elements of Henry's commentary were informed by his knowledge of Hebrew and had the support of ancient tradition.

Henry's comments on v. 12 provide a helpful degree of clarity to this prayer for instruction in numbering one's days in order to gain a heart of wisdom. The psalm as a whole is a prayer for daily meditation on the part of the wilderness generation. They were to pray for instruction to number their days of punishment so that they might gain wisdom from the circumstances that led to the punishment. One might ask what benefit gaining wisdom would be if they are nevertheless condemned to die in the wilderness. The answer is found in the narrative setting of the wilderness tradition and in the prayer of v. 16 for the children of the praying community. The wisdom to be gained from numbering the days of judgment is to be passed on to the succeeding generation, who will inherit the promised land.

The appeal of Henry's teaching on Psalm 90 needs to be weighed against its limitations. Although the connection to the story in Numbers 14 has benefits, there is no evidence within the text that requires this setting for the prayer. In fact, there is one significant tension between Numbers 14 and Psalm 90. The confession of sin in v. 8 states, "You have set our iniquities before you, our secret sins in the light of your countenance." However, the transgression of the people in Numbers 14 was not a secret sin but rather a public act. They rejected the report of the spies that was in agreement with the divine promise of possessing the land. A second point of tension is in the statement of v. 10, that "the days of our life are seventy years, or perhaps eighty, if we are strong." Even allowing for the poetic language of the prayer, and for the symbolic use of the numbers 70 and 80, the prayer is in conflict with both the biblical story of Moses, whose life span is reckoned at 120 years, and with the ages of the generation of the exodus. The youngest members of that generation were 20 years old, and their punishment was set specifically at 40 years, "according to the number of the days in which you spied out the land, forty days, for every day a year, you shall bear your iniquity, forty years" (Num 14:34). These tensions between the psalm and the narrative setting proposed by Henry are similar to tensions in other psalms with headings that reference historical people or events from biblical narratives. These tensions suggest that headings like the one in Psalm 90, "the prayer of Moses," are just that—headings that are not intended to provide historical clues about the origins of the psalm.

The primary weaknesses of Henry's reading of Psalm 90, however valuable it is for devotional study, are the narrow scope of his writing within a brief commentary on the whole Bible and the limited knowledge of the language, culture, and history of ancient Israel available during the time in which he lived. In the two centuries after Henry's commentary, revolutionary discoveries would be made in ancient Near Eastern language, literature, and history. In addition, a transformation in the intellectual environment and perspective of Western culture created radical shifts in the understanding and interpretation of religious texts and traditions. These profound changes produced new critical methods and interpretations of the Bible. The new approaches can be illustrated by an example of the critical reading of Psalm 90 found in the commentary published in 1906–1907 by Charles Augustus Briggs in *The International Critical Commentary on the Holy Scriptures of the Old and New Testaments*.[16]

In his book about the history of the interpretation of the Psalms, Old Testament scholar William L. Holladay highlighted Briggs's career and commentary as a milestone in the critical approach to the Psalms.[17] The two hundred years between Matthew Henry's commentary and that of Briggs witnessed a revolution in Western civilization. The eighteenth-century Age of Enlightenment elevated the authority of reason, science, and individual liberty over the traditional authorities of church doctrine and absolute monarchy. Holladay identified key events of the nineteenth century as catalysts for the work of Briggs and others. These include the discovery and deciphering of ancient texts from Egypt, Mesopotamia, and Persia that illuminate the cultural and historical background of ancient Israel. Also, in the mid-1800s, the works of Charles Lyell in geology and Charles Darwin in biology introduced the idea of identifiable stages of historical development into the study of all subjects ranging from the natural sciences to the humanities, including world religions, literature, and history.[18] The influence and results of this intellectual revolution are well represented in Briggs's career and commentary.

Briggs studied under Edward Robinson, a German-trained American scholar who was a pioneer in both the archaeology of Palestine and the historical study of Hebrew and ancient Near Eastern languages. Briggs continued his studies in Germany, where he embraced and mastered the historical-critical method of biblical interpretation. This method sought to peel back the later stages of development underlying the received form of the biblical text and to reveal the original form of the text and the historical setting in which it was first composed. He became a leading figure in American biblical scholarship as a professor at Union Theological Seminary, partly through the notoriety of his trial for heresy and expulsion from the Presbyterian Church, but mostly due to his immense contributions to biblical scholarship. He was one of the three English translators, along with Francis Brown and Samuel R. Driver, of William Gesenius's Hebrew-German lexicon, a translation that came to be known as the Brown-Driver-Briggs lexicon. He was also a principal editor, along with Driver and Alfred Plummer, of the International Critical Commentary on the Bible. His commentary on the Psalms, published with his daughter Emilie Grace Briggs in two volumes in 1906 and 1907, is a useful example of the critical study of Psalm 90.

Briggs's commentary was a work of enormous erudition. He wrote in the preface that he had worked on the critical interpretation of the Psalms for forty years. The commentary included textual analysis that sought to identify the best Hebrew text of the Psalms by "detection and elimination of glosses."[19] In his view, scribal additions and explanations had crept into the Hebrew text during its long transmission and required critical methods in order to identify and remove them. This methodology involved comparison of the Hebrew text and the major ancient translations, including the

Greek, Aramaic, and Latin versions. He also sought to identify the original text by reconstructing the poetry of the Psalms, believing that the original contained lines of balanced meter and strophes of equal lines similar to classical Greek and Latin poetry. (Contemporary study of Hebrew poetry no longer presumes that ancient Hebrew poetry had a consistent pattern of meter or strophic structure, and scholars today are much less willing to eliminate textual material for poetic reasons.) Briggs also attempted to identify the date of composition of each psalm through literary and historical criticism, and to make his commentary compatible with the latest findings in the areas of biblical theology and interpretation. While his study was the result of impressive scholarship, it was far from the picture Griffiths created of a religious reader who was intrinsically equipped to read the sacred text. Briggs admitted, after forty years of study, that "If I could spend more years in preparation, doubtless I would do much better work."[20]

Briggs described Psalm 90 as a communal prayer for the people of Israel as a whole. Its perspective looked back on Israel's long history from a condition of affliction that it interpreted as the result of divine anger at the nation's sin, a condition that had continued for a long time.[21] Certain literary clues, like the spelling of the Hebrew word used for "heart" in v. 12 and similarities to Jeremiah, Isaiah 40–55, and Ezekiel, suggested a historical setting in the late exilic period, around the middle of the sixth century BCE. Briggs labeled the title, "the prayer of Moses," as a pseudograph. A pseudograph is an attribution of a text to a legendary figure in order to lend the figure's authority to a new literary composition. Briggs recognized literary connections in Psalm 90 with Pentateuchal traditions like Deuteronomy 32–33 and Genesis 2–3, but he judged them to be intentional efforts on the part of the anonymous author to provide support for the attribution to Moses.

Briggs divided the psalm into six units of relatively equal length (after he had eliminated scribal additions). He interpreted its message in the context of Israel's situation in exile. The affirmation of the LORD in v. 1 as the dwelling place of Israel was similar to the description of God in Ezekiel 11 as "a sanctuary" for the exiles after their removal from Jerusalem. He read v. 3 in accordance with the Greek translation to say "(Do not) turn man back to dust; and say: 'Return, ye sons of mankind.'" He saw this as a plea that the nation of Israel not be sentenced to death in the way that Adam and Eve were sentenced to die for their sin in Genesis 3:19. The 1,000 years mentioned in v. 4 were taken as a reference to Israel's history.

Though 1,000 years is a long time in human perspective, it is only a day to God. The argument was that Israel's life was too short to end in exile.

Briggs connected the image in v. 5 of the grass that flourishes in the morning but withers in the afternoon with the confession of Israel's sin in v. 8 through the shared imagery of sunlight. The sunlight of God's face that beheld Israel's sin threatened to bring them to an end like the desert sun that withered the morning grass. God's wrath, if unabated, threatened the future existence of the people: "[Our lives] are soon gone, and we fly away" (v. 10). The prayers of vv. 12-17 were a response to this threat.

Briggs's translation of v. 12 is especially disappointing for my quest to understand what it means to "count our days that we may gain a wise heart." He changed the text so that it reads as something else entirely! He changed the vowels of the Hebrew word translated "our days" so that he could read it as a similar Hebrew word meaning "your right hand." His translation is "Thy hand so make us know that we may get a heart of wisdom." "Thy hand" is the heavy hand of God's punishment, described in vv. 7-11. Verse 12 is a prayer for wisdom to learn the lesson of divine punishment and learn how to live properly before God.[22] The remainder of the psalm is a prayer that God will meet Israel's repentance with mercy so that they may rejoice and be glad for as many days as they have known affliction. Psalm 90 prays for a time when the measure of Israel's punishment in the exile will be fulfilled, an idea of proportional judgment similar to the one described in Isaiah 40:2. Briggs's text of Psalm 90 ends at v. 15 because he judged vv. 16-17 to be interpretive glosses added to the original poem at a later date.

Briggs's interpretation of the psalm presents it as a plaintive prayer of Israel in response to the affliction of the Babylonian exile, couched in the voice of Moses, Israel's greatest teacher. The prayer confesses God, not the lost temple or the land, as Israel's true dwelling place. It appeals for mercy so that Israel's brief life in the eyes of God will not end in exile. It confesses Israel's sin and the appropriateness of God's wrath, and it asks for wisdom to know how to change one's ways. Finally, it asks for mercy in response to the hard lessons the people have learned through affliction. Briggs's interpretation is thematically consistent and poetically balanced, composed of six poetic units of five lines each. His interpretation of the nation of Israel as the focus of the prayer throughout gives the psalm a degree of coherence and unity.

Although modern scholars would take issue with many of the finer points of Briggs's interpretation, his comments have one major flaw above all others. The psalm that he described in his commentary does not exist anywhere outside his commentary! Words and phrases that did not fit his reconstruction of the "original" poem were eliminated from the psalm. The text of Briggs's reconstructed psalm is based in most cases on the Greek translator's understanding of his Hebrew text. Contemporary textual criticism is much more skeptical of the value of the Greek translation of the Psalms when compared to the major witnesses of the Hebrew textual tradition. Briggs, however, favored the readings of the Greek tradition in almost every case. Briggs's interpretation has a strong degree of unity partly due not only to his careful literary observations but also to the fact that he eliminated material that did not fit his interpretation. The interpretation, therefore, has a kind of circular logic. Briggs defined the topic and meaning of the psalm, then eliminated from the text elements of the psalm that did not fit the topic and meaning he had defined.

How does Briggs's interpretation compare with that of Matthew Henry? It is important to note that in spite of the differences in historical setting and the aims of their respective works, their readings do share some things in common. Both readings demonstrate great learning and deep study of the psalm. Henry was familiar with the Hebrew text and also with traditions of interpretation drawn from patristic, Reformation, and medieval Jewish sources. Briggs had mastered all of the major ancient versions and also the most important scholarly literature on the psalm in Germany, England, and America. Although their results differ, both writers emphasize the importance of identifying the historical setting for the psalm. Henry located it in the wilderness period while Briggs located it during the exile. Although these periods are centuries apart, metaphorically they are similar. The wilderness narratives have served as a frequent metaphor for Israel's exilic and postexilic history since the time of exile itself.

On the specific text of v. 12 at the center of my interest in Psalm 90, Henry and Briggs agree on its essential meaning. Both see the text as a prayer that the people will gain valuable wisdom from their painful experience of divine punishment. This agreement is remarkable given the fact that they understood the punishment as a result of very different circumstances and also given the fact that Briggs changed the wording of the verse from the wording of the text used by Henry. The two authors also agree on the general cause of the struggle to cope with the nature of time expressed in the psalm as a whole, although again their understandings of the specific contexts are very different. Both see the complaint about the difficulty of making wise use of time as a result of a specific experience of divine

punishment. For Henry it was the punishment of the wilderness generation; for Briggs it was the Babylonian exile.

Although there are similarities between them, the differences between
Henry and Briggs are clear and significant. Each reading clearly reflects the
primary aims and settings of its author. Henry, a pastor, wanted to make the
religious meaning of the text available and applicable to Christian readers.
His assumption was that a well-equipped teacher could make the riches of
meaning within the text accessible and relatable to receptive people of faith.
The downside of Henry's focus is that several questions that were raised by
details of the text could not be addressed satisfactorily or even cursorily
within the limits set by his approach. Even if his project had allowed time
and space for dealing with critical issues, information and methodologies
helpful for doing so were not available to Henry in his day.

Briggs's aim was not to address religious readers directly, but rather to
produce a definitive reference guide for scholars, teachers, and students of
Psalm 90 that would trace the historical development of the psalm back to
an original text and an original meaning. Important resources for doing
this had emerged from archaeology, history, literary criticism, and comparative linguistics. The goal of seeking an original text and meaning arrived
at by scientific methods served a higher goal of providing neutral ground
on which religious disputes might be resolved. The price of establishing
such neutral ground, however, was to mediate the authority of the text
through the authority of scholars like Briggs. Briggs thought that the original text had been so corrupted by its religious use that only an expert
such as himself could restore it. The irony of Briggs's approach is that his
method assumed that the religious use of the text as authoritative Scripture
had led to the corruption of the text's original authoritative form. As a
result, the authority of the text was dependent on the authority of scholars
like himself to correct what religious communities had marred. For Briggs,
the authority of the original text had to be saved from the results of its
long use as an authoritative text. In contrast to Henry's religious reading,
which saw the text as a rich reserve of potential meanings, Briggs's approach
sought a single meaning based on the reconstruction of an original form
and setting that had been lost centuries ago—in fact, not long after it was
first circulated.

The different goals of the two readings led to different uses of Psalm
90. Henry's commentary leads to direct religious instructions for his
reader about how one ought to think, feel, believe, act, and pray based
on the content of the psalm. Briggs's commentary calls primarily for an

informed appreciation of the text on the part of his readers. Readers should understand the original form and meaning of the text and appreciate the artfulness of its poetry and the thoughtfulness of its religious ideas. Briggs gives no instruction as to what the reader should do in response to Psalm 90. In fact, it is not clear that the reader should do anything with Psalm 90 at all, other than perhaps pray when facing a similiar situation.

By the time of Briggs's commentary on Psalms, the critical approach to reading the Bible was gaining strength in academic institutions, and, by the middle of the twentieth century, it became the dominant the way to teach and study the Bible in schools and seminaries. At the same time, religious reading continued in churches and denominational educational programs and among religious writers and individual readers. Over the course of the twentieth century, the two approaches influenced each other. Religious readings of Scripture incorporated more of the historical and linguistic information coming out of discoveries from archaeology and ancient Near Eastern history. Many of the scholars who practiced and taught the critical reading of Scripture continued to come from religious communities and to serve those communities as teachers, writers, and ministers. In fact, as Jon Levenson has pointed out, the critical study of the Bible is deeply dependent on religious communities, both for the students who desire to study the Bible and for the readers willing to purchase the literature that scholars produce about the Bible.[23] Not surprisingly, secular students and readers are not overly interested in the critical histories of texts whose original historical meaning must be traced back to people and places far, far away and long, long ago. A further irony is that the religious motivation to learn about the Bible is so great that members of religious communities are the primary audience for critical readings of the Bible, even though those readings approach the text with the assumption that religious views are an obstacle to understanding the texts correctly.

CONCLUSION: THE NEED TO INTEGRATE RELIGIOUS AND CRITICAL READINGS OF SCRIPTURE

An examination of the two primary ways of approaching Psalm 90 and other biblical texts shows that each approach has its own strengths and limitations. Religious reading is able to find a deep treasury of meaning within the text that is available to a wide audience of religious readers. It often avoids or suppresses elements of the text that are in tension with its goals or results. It can miss out on useful information that is beyond the scope of knowledge of the broad religious community as a whole. Further, its focus on the needs of religious communities can isolate religious readers from the insights, concerns, and even correction of communities of readers outside its boundaries.

Critical reading, on the other hand, seeks to bring the best resources of human knowledge, reason, and discovery to bear on understanding the Bible. It often finds helpful solutions to textual puzzles that are dependent on a history of the text that has been lost in its transmission. It also tries to calm conflicts between various readers by elevating a single reading, most frequently a reconstructed "original" meaning, as the most authoritative one. The price of identifying this single meaning, however, is to marginalize the traditions of the very reading communities who have preserved the Bible, and to reduce a rich array of meanings to a time-bound one that is available only through the mediation of an elite group of scholars.

Although religious reading and critical reading are the two most commonly accepted approaches to reading Psalm 90, they are not the only approaches available. Over the past thirty years, scholars in the fields of biblical studies, church history, and Christian theology have been seeking ways to bring together the strengths of each approach while minimizing their respective limitations. The results of these efforts represent a new approach to biblical studies broadly referred to as the theological inter-pretation of Scripture. The theological interpretation of Scripture is not a methodology for studying the Bible as much as a set of goals and practices that aims to bridge the divisions between church and academy, between biblical studies and theology, and between scholars and informed readers of the Bible in religious communities. Theological interpretation shows that there are benefits of combining religious and critical readings of the Bible. I want to introduce one promising model of the theological interpretation of Scripture and apply it to understanding Psalm 90. In doing so, I hope not only to further my quest to learn how to count my days that I might gain a wise heart but also to demonstrate how people of faith can use the best of religious and critical approaches to the study of Scripture for the purposes of Christian faith and discipleship.

Chapter 2

Four Conversations:
A Model for Theological
Interpretation of Scripture

Interpretations of the Bible generally fall into one of two primary approaches: religious reading and critical reading. Although these two patterns of reading share some common features, they tend to be practiced separately from one another, with religious reading taking place primarily in churches and personal devotions, and critical reading holding sway in schools and academic writing. Christian ministers, however, must navigate both approaches.

Through teaching students in a doctor of ministry program, I have seen firsthand the challenges ministers face in bridging the two major approaches to interpreting the Bible. Doctor of ministry students are practicing ministers who have a basic theological degree and are pursuing advanced research in ministry leadership. They are familiar with the patterns of religious reading that take place primarily in congregations and in personal devotional practice. Religious reading was the first way they learned to read the Bible, and it is the primary way most people in their congregations still read the Bible. As a result of their graduate-level study in seminary or divinity school, these minister-students are also familiar with the practices of critical reading that take place primarily in academic settings. They have learned the major findings and essential tools of critical biblical studies.

When DMin students enter my class on interpreting biblical texts for the practice of ministry, they have been serving in full-time, vocational ministry for at least three years. During that time, they have been trying to integrate the critical approach they learned in school with the religious approach that they first used to read the Bible and that is practiced by many people in their congregations. They find that an exclusively critical approach helps to resolve some of the puzzles presented by the biblical text and may satisfy the intellectual struggles of some in their congregations. They are also aware, however, that critical reading alone does not address many people's spiritual and existential needs for an awareness of God's presence and a sense of purpose and guidance in their lives. If they have gained the skills and managed the methods needed to trace a biblical text back to its likely meaning at the time of its historical origins, they then face the challenge of bringing that message back into the twenty-first century to connect with the lives of people living in a very different world.[24]

If my DMin students feel dissatisfied with a strictly critical reading of the Bible, they have also recognized that a purely religious reading leaves many questions unanswered. They have learned enough of the ancient context and historical origins of the Bible to know that it should not be read with the same expectations of direct understanding as the daily newspaper or a current blog post. They find that critical study can be useful for explaining puzzling texts and for debunking the most extreme views of the Bible that lay readers present to them. They also sense, however, that the work of ministry needs to be more than the work of debunking. Most of these ministers develop their own improvisational style of blending religious and critical reading that works in their contexts. When they return to school for their postgraduate degrees, however, many express anxiety that their way of improvising the relationship between religious and critical reading will not meet the standards of academic biblical studies. They feel they have to go back, temporarily, to following "the rules of the school" rather than the method of interpretation they have learned in their ministry praxis.

This book proposes a model of theological interpretation that combines the best of religious and critical approaches to reading the Bible. Before introducing the model, however, I will describe the advantages of the most frequently used critical approach to the Bible, the historical-critical method. I will then describe the reasons that this approach has lost some of the dominance it enjoyed in the mid- to late twentieth century and also why other approaches have been proposed to supplement or even replace it. This discussion will pave the way for a description of an alternative approach that offers Christian ministers, leaders, and students greater potential for fulfilling the goals they have for reading the Bible.

THE NECESSITY AND BENEFITS OF HISTORICAL-CRITICAL INTERPRETATION OF THE BIBLE

The previous chapter compared the religious reading of Psalm 90 by Matthew Henry with the critical approach of Charles Augustus Briggs. Although my comparison highlighted strengths and weaknesses of each approach, there has been no comparison between the two in terms of their influence on biblical studies since the publication of Briggs's commentary in 1906. The critical approach pioneered in America by Briggs and others became the dominant way of interpreting the Bible for the remainder of the twentieth century in the domains of higher education, academic publishing, and professional scholarly organizations. Over the last thirty years, however, recognition of the limitations of historical criticism have led to the development of new approaches to interpreting the Bible and also to the reevaluation of older approaches.

Historical-critical study of the Bible is based on assumptions about the nature of the Bible as a literary text that can be studied and understood in ways that are similar to any other text. These assumptions inform the way scholars approach the Bible. Although the assumptions are reasonable and widely shared, it is helpful to name them in order to understand the rise and lasting appeal of this approach to the Bible.

1. *Historical-critical study assumes that biblical texts were composed in specific historical, cultural, and linguistic contexts and therefore are best understood in relation to those contexts.* This assumption seems obvious, but because the Bible has been translated and transmitted across many centuries and in many settings, the influence of the original setting can be harder to detect in translation and therefore is often overlooked. Historical-critical study pays attention to the role of the original context in shaping the unique features of the text. Often, textual features that pose difficulty for contemporary readers can be resolved by reference to what is known about the text's historical background.

2. *The historical-critical method assumes that careful study is able to discover or reconstruct the original contexts and intent of the Bible accurately enough to create a reasonable and reliable interpretation.* The world that produced the unique features of the Bible is far removed in time and understanding from the world of the contemporary reader. Nevertheless, scholarship has discovered a great deal of information about the ancient world and its history, languages, cultures, and literature. Historical-critical study is based on the judgment that modern reconstructions of the world

"behind the text" are sufficient to help modern people understand the original meaning of biblical texts.

3. *Historical-critical study assumes that the process of discovering the original intent of the words of the Bible in their original contexts is the necessary first step to good interpretation.* This assumption may again seem obvious in light of the other assumptions stated above, but it is an assumption that is subject to question and debate. The reason for questioning this assumption is the nature and function of the Bible as a religious text used for religious purposes in the context of a faith community. For believing communities, the Bible contains religious meanings that transcend the context and circumstances of its origin. After all, if this were not the case, then it would be hard to explain why the Bible would have been transmitted beyond the earliest generations of people who understood its meaning in the original setting. If a text did not speak to circumstances beyond its original audience, its meaning would eventually have been lost to succeeding generations. Leaders of the Protestant Reformation referred to this aspect of the Bible as "the perspicuity of Scripture." This term means that the believing community, though at some distance from the original context, can nevertheless read the Bible with an understanding of its primary message. The assumptions of the historical-critical approach imply that special expertise in historical studies is required in order to understand the Bible rightly. Although there is tension between the religious use and the historical use of the Bible, it is possible to see both approaches as possessing truth. Millions of people worldwide read the Bible for religious purposes and derive meaning from their reading without special historical training. At the same time, scholars trained in critical study reveal historical dimensions of meaning in context based on in-depth study. Though the religious and literary readers and historically oriented readers often conflict with one another on the question of which approach is best, there is a consensus that the meaning of a text in its historical context, where this can reasonably be identified, is an important starting point for interpretation. The historical context provides a sense of "givenness" to the text that serves as a limit to the range of possible meanings, while also providing a common starting point for readers from different perspectives.

Many benefits have resulted from following the assumptions and methodologies of the historical-critical approach to the Bible. For the essential elements of biblical study, such as identifying and translating the best-preserved text of a biblical passage, historical-critical studies are indispensable. Critical study is also beneficial in solving some of the hardest-to-understand elements of biblical language for modern readers. Many biblical idioms and figures of speech are embedded in the linguistic and cultural patterns of the ancient Near East or the Greco-Roman world. Historical study makes these phenomena of Scripture understandable.

In addition to solving puzzles caused by ancient language, historical-critical study also provides a kind of control mechanism or even a corrective to speculative, self-interested, or prejudicial interpretations or applications of biblical texts. Severed from their original context, the words of Scripture can be twisted into meanings far from their intended use, giving biblical authority to the personal agendas of individuals or groups. Historical-critical study can provide some degree of protection against erroneous or abusive readings of the Bible.

Beyond the role of correcting poor interpretations, historical-critical study can provide helpful points of contact between ancient audiences and contemporary readers. While cultures change across time, historical readings of the Bible can reveal concrete points of identification between experiences in the ancient world and today. Experiences such as political oppression, social injustice, the horrors of war, family joys and sorrows, and the shared emotions and conditions of human nature across time and cultures are often highlighted by historical study. The original contexts of the Bible often illustrate points of continuity in human nature and provide numerous connections with situations in contemporary life.

While the common points of contact between the biblical world and today are helpful, perhaps even more important are the elements of difference and even strangeness between the Bible and contemporary culture that are highlighted by historical study. The differences between the biblical world and our own can provide an opportunity for comparison and evaluation, a chance to step outside the bubble of modern life and see it imaginatively through the lens of a different culture and set of values. Theologian Karl Barth argued that the strangeness of the Bible was part of its power to address modern people as "the strange world of the word of God." Historical-critical study can demonstrate and emphasize this difference in ways that provide a challenge and a correction to uncritical assumptions of a modern worldview.

The gains in knowledge produced by critical biblical scholarship are hard to overstate. The histories of the ancient Near East and the Greco-Roman world have been painstakingly mapped out, and the people, events, movements, and literary forms of the Bible have been carefully located against this historical backdrop. The deciphering of ancient languages, unknown for centuries, and the translation and study of ancient texts have provided a rich contextual environment for reading biblical literature with greater clarity and depth. Peoples, states, civilizations, and cultures of the Bible that before were merely names on a page have taken on color and vividness as three-dimensional characters in the biblical drama. The literary richness of the Bible—its sagas, songs, speeches, and sayings—can be heard against the background of the cultural lexicon and repertoire of its time.

THE LIMITATIONS OF HISTORICAL-CRITICAL STUDY

As a biblical scholar, I celebrate the benefits that critical study of the Bible has brought to our ability to read Scripture with depth, richness, and understanding. The benefits of critical study, however, have not been without some cost for reading and teaching the Bible as Holy Scripture for the spiritual guidance of believing communities. In recent decades, the historical-critical approach to biblical studies has come full circle as scholars have applied critical tools and sensibilities to the methods, results, and aims of critical scholarship itself. As a result, a new awareness of the limitations and negative repercussions of historical-critical study now balances out the ledger of its many contributions.

One of the weaknesses of historical-critical study is a focus on the history behind the biblical text to the detriment of attention to the text itself. There is a great deal of direct and comparative evidence for the fact that many biblical texts are the result of multiple stages of composition, expansion, and revision over time.[25] This should be no surprise given the great antiquity of the Bible and its long history of transmission across many generations. Historical-critical study, however, has often given priority to the earliest stages of the text's growth to the neglect of the literary form in which it has been passed down to contemporary readers. Following an archaeological model, historical-critical study has often treated elements of the text that seemed to be later additions as so much dirt to be removed in order to discover the earlier and, by assumption, more important stages of composition. As demonstrated in Briggs's interpretation of Psalm 90, his reconstruction of the "original" text of the psalm produced a version that exists nowhere outside of his commentary. The form of Psalm 90 that had been received through the history of transmission had become an obstacle for the proper reading of the "original" text, or at least Briggs's reconstruction of it.

Another limitation of historical criticism is the idea that a text of the Bible has only one meaning, which is the meaning that it had in its historical context for its original author and audience. This idea was espoused in an important essay by Benjamin Jowett titled "On the Interpretation of Scripture." Jowett famously wrote, "Scripture has one meaning—the meaning which it had to the mind of the Prophet or Evangelist who first uttered or wrote, to the hearers or readers who first received it."[26] Coupled with this idea of the single original meaning is the view that this meaning can be determined by objective methods and recognized as true for all reasonable interpreters. While the idea of identifying the one meaning of Scripture by objective measures agreeable to all based on a universal reason sounds appealing, in practice it has often been an unachievable goal. One significant mark against critical scholarship's claim of objectivity is the multiplication of numerous "objective" interpretations that have been offered for the finite set of texts within the Bible. The literature of critical biblical scholarship contains copious arguments for widely varying views on the date, authorship, audience, and aims of biblical texts. The many conflicts arising from multiple interpretations discredit claims of objectivity.

Upon reflection, the idea that the single meaning of a Scripture text is the one it had for its original author and audience prompts the question of why anyone not living in the time and circumstances of the original setting would be interested in a meaning that belongs to the distant past. The vast majority of writings of the past did not survive beyond the age of their original audience. In order to survive through multiple generations, a text must continue to speak in new ways to new contexts. This reality does not negate the value of an original, historical meaning, but it does require the recognition of multiple meanings of a text in multiple contexts over time. This was the primary argument of David Steinmetz in a famous essay titled "The Superiority of Pre-Critical Exegesis."[27] Steinmetz compared historical-critical scholarship's attempts to communicate the meaning of biblical texts to the medieval church's concept of the multiple levels of meaning or "senses" of the text. Through attention to the literal, spiritual, moral, and eschatological levels of meaning, ancient spiritual exegesis could address the full tradition of the text's transmission, past and present. His conclusion was that "the medieval theory of levels of meaning in the biblical text, with all its undoubted defects, flourished because it is true, while the modern theory of a single meaning, with all its demonstrable virtues, is false."[28]

Investigation of the historical and cultural origins of critical biblical scholarship has suggested that, far from being purely objective, critical scholarship grew out of a very distinct, politically motivated set of circumstances. Historians Scott Hahn and Benjamin Wiker marshaled substantial evidence in support of the thesis that the historical-critical approach emerged from the political tensions in Europe between the church and the emerging nation-states in the late medieval, Renaissance, and Reformation eras. Critical biblical scholarship was aided throughout its history by allied forces of secularization seeking to wrest political control from ecclesial authority.[29] This history does not discredit the benefits of critical scholarship. The historical context of historical criticism, however, does reveal something of the political motivations for its claim to objective truth. One factor in the rise of the historical-critical approach was its roots in a power struggle in Western history between the institution of the academy and the institution of the church.

ALTERNATIVE APPROACHES TO HISTORICAL CRITICISM

The limitations of historical-critical approaches to the Bible provoked criticism from within and from beyond the guild of biblical scholarship in the last decades of the twentieth century. As voices from political movements such as feminist, liberationist, and postcolonial criticism gained greater standing in academic biblical scholarship, further critique of the underlying interests and power structures of historical-critical scholarship emerged. In her presidential address to the Society of Biblical Literature in 1981 titled "The Ethics of Biblical Interpretation," New Testament scholar Elisabeth Schüssler Fiorenza argued that the accepted methods and conclusions of critical scholarship often served as a gatekeeping function for cultivating and maintaining a guild of scholars that shared a common demographic background.[30] Rather than attempting a false objectivity that masked the favoring of one privileged group, she argued that biblical scholarship should become "scholarship for" the interests of politically marginalized groups. Other scholars in the 1980s and 1990s promoted the use of critical literary theories such as deconstruction and postcolonial theory as ways to challenge a form of rationalism in traditional scholarship that they saw as a legitimization for the unequal power arrangements of imperialist and colonialist interests. Scholars from nations that had been colonized by Western powers called specific attention to the role of the Bible and biblical scholarship in legitimizing Western colonization and oppression of indigenous peoples in Africa, South America, and South Asia.[31] The common thread uniting liberationist, feminist, and postcolonial criticism is the claim that the goals and conclusions of historical-critical study of the Bible were not based on objective and purely rational criteria alone, but rather served the political and economic interests of certain people at the expense of many others.

These challenges to the results and motives of historical criticism led to the emergence of new methodologies influenced by literary theory, political theory, the social sciences, and a variety of perspectival approaches that situate interpretation within the concrete experiences of specific identity groups. The experiences and perspectives of scholars from diverse backgrounds have broadened, enriched, and also challenged the interpretation of the Bible. One result of the proliferation of approaches to biblical interpretation has been the further fragmentation of the already highly specialized field of biblical studies. The diversity of approaches and subspecialties within the field has served to create even greater distance between the academic study of the Bible and the general reading public.

The tendency of historical criticism to distance the biblical text from the concerns and interpretations of contemporary communities has had a far-reaching effect. This effect came home to me in a jarring way in a church-based adult Bible study class. The teacher of the Bible study, a layperson with a seminary degree, summarized the operating assumption of the historical-critical approach in stark terms. In his introductory remarks about the biblical text being discussed, he told the highly educated and successful adults participating in the class that they "*could not possibly* understand the text without the aid of professional scholars" (emphasis added). This teacher had internalized the often unspoken curriculum of critical biblical scholarship that interpretations outside the methods of historical criticism are not valid. If religious readers cannot understand the text without submitting to a method of interpretation that devalues the literary context of the biblical canon as a reliable guide to its meaning, what religious benefit can they gain from it?

This tension between the assumptions and goals of historical criticism and the needs of religious communities was noted decades ago by James D. Smart in his book *The Strange Silence of the Bible in the Church*.[32] Smart observed in 1970 that in spite of the greatest volume of information about the Bible that had ever been compiled in human history, the Bible was read in the church with less frequency, understanding, and authority than ever before. Among the many causes, he focused specifically on the hermeneutical weakness of the historical-critical approach. This method led readers into a painstakingly recreated past, located in a time before the text was part of the Bible, but with little guidance for how to bring the historically contextualized text back into conversation with the present day. Since the appearance of Smart's book in 1970, the Bible has become even more silent, though the silence has become less and less strange.

In response to the limitations of historical-critical scholarship, academic interpretation of the Bible has expanded within the last thirty years to include the experiences and contributions of multiple populations and multiple points of view.[33] As a result of this expansion, a space has also opened in the academy for conscious interpretation of the Bible on behalf of people of faith who read the Bible within a believing and worshiping community whose history spans millennia. This approach is called the theological interpretation of Scripture. Although theological interpretation has been practiced continually in churches throughout Christian history and also in confessional groups active within the academy, one of the marks of contemporary theological interpretation is the awareness of the current, postcritical moment. It would be wrong to say that the study of the Bible has returned full circle to the primarily confessional interpretation of the precritical era. Theological exegesis is only one approach to the Bible among many approaches in the contemporary, pluralistic academy, rather than the dominant approach that it once was prior to the modern period. Nevertheless, the strong grip of the atomizing, historicist methodologies of interpretation that dominated biblical studies for nearly two centuries has given way to a plethora of new methods. This methodological diversity has provided space for informed, reflective, consciously theological interpretations of Old and New Testament texts as Christian Scripture. What are the features of the approach known as theological interpretation?

WHAT IS THEOLOGICAL INTERPRETATION OF SCRIPTURE?

In the past thirty years, scholars in the fields of biblical studies, Christian theology, and church history have been practicing renewed forms of reading the Bible as divine revelation in human language within the framework affirmed by the Christian church in its historic, ecumenical creeds. The impetus for this renewal has come from biblical scholars who find their identity as Christians to be relevant to the texts they study, from theologians who see biblical interpretation as an integral part of the discipline of theology, and from church historians who do not privilege the modern period of biblical study as the ultimate measure of good biblical interpretation.

The recent rise of theological interpretation as a topic of research can be attested in many ways. For example, in 2009 when Michael Gorman revised his 2004 textbook *Elements of Biblical Exegesis*, enough research had emerged on the topic of theological interpretation in just five years to allow him to add an entirely new chapter and expanded bibliography on the topic of theological exegesis.[34] Multiple introductions to theological interpretation have appeared in the past ten years.[35] New theological commentary series have also appeared, such as the Brazos Theological Commentary on the Bible, The Church's Bible, and Belief: A Theological Commentary on the Bible. During the same period, a dictionary of theological interpretation has been written and a new academic journal, *The Journal of Theological Interpretation*, has also appeared.[36]

What are the major hallmarks of this renewed theological approach to the Bible in the academy? In a chapter on theological interpretation in his handbook of biblical exegesis, Gorman stated that there is a broad consensus among practitioners that theological interpretation is not a specific method of study added to the list of other methodologies practiced within biblical scholarship.[37] Many see the emphasis on method in the academy as part of a rhetorical claim to objectivity that masked scholars' personal interests and commitments. Practitioners of theological interpretation describe it as a set of dispositions and goals rather than a specific methodology. Theological interpretation involves a set of convictions about the role of the Bible in Christian life and a set of practices of reading that grow out of these convictions. While they are described in various ways in the literature on theological exegesis, these dispositions and goals can be summarized under the rubrics of communion, church, critical study, canon, and creed.

Communion

Communion refers to the religious and spiritual dimensions of Scripture reading and to the worship life of the faith communities who revere the Bible as a source for divine revelation. The goal of communion accepts that God may address readers of the Bible through the providentially ordered gift of Scripture. Rather than seeing the Bible as evidence to be used in recreating the history of its literary development or the times and cultures in which it was produced, theological interpretation reads the Bible with an openness to receiving communication from God and experiencing communion with God. Receiving divine communication through Scripture is a spiritual experience. Stephen Fowl locates the understanding of the Bible as a vehicle for communion in the Christian confession of God as existing in eternal community within the persons of the Holy Trinity and seeking communion beyond the divine life through acts of creation and self-disclosure.[38] One of the major themes of the Bible is a pervasive state of alienation between God and creation, and especially between God and humankind. In the context of alienation, communion with God through God's self-revelation in creation and in history, mediated through Israel and Jesus, is a redemptive and transformative experience. To the degree that communion with God addresses the alienation that is at the heart of human discord and brokenness, it should lead to renewed communion with the neighbor as well. In one of the earliest works in the recent renewal of theological interpretation, Fowl describes the primary aim of theological interpretation to be reading the Bible in such a way as to foster greater communion with God and others.[39]

The idea of communion as a goal of biblical interpretation includes an openness to the Bible as a vehicle of divine communication. In mysterious yet discernible ways, God communicates through the human words of the Bible, transforming the Bible into the word of God that addresses and transforms fallen people living in a fallen world. Reading Scripture with an openness to being addressed by God encourages certain virtues of reading such as yielding to divine guidance, giving attention to the presence of God, nurturing an attitude of trust in the divine will as disclosed through the biblical word, and cultivating an openness toward the Other, who is also a potential recipient and vehicle for divine communication.[40]

Church

Throughout most of its history, the spiritual practice of reading the Bible for the goal of communion with God has taken place within the context of worshiping communities. Although every religious tradition has within it a strand of mysticism that emphasizes the individual's union with the divine, Christian theological interpretation focuses primarily on the believing community, the church, as the primary location of the work of biblical interpretation. Part of this emphasis grows naturally out of the role of the Bible in the worshiping life of the church. Another part comes from the long tradition of church-oriented interpretation across the span of Christian history. Indeed, one of the goals of theological interpretation is to reacquaint the church with the long and rich tradition of interpretation of the Bible preserved in church history.[41] The communal context includes not only the contemporary congregational setting but also the historical community of saints and saintly interpreters of past generations.[42]

The focus on the ecclesial context of biblical interpretation is necessary because of the peculiar history of Western universities and scholarly guilds. European universities were early sites of resistance to the church's dominance of the intellectual tradition of western Europe. Historical-critical studies were one way that Western intellectuals sought to free society from an ecclesiastically controlled view of the world based on the church's exclusive authority in interpreting Scripture. Historical criticism developed in an environment in which objective study of the Bible had to be freed from the political power of ecclesiastical interpretation. Theological interpretation seeks to reorient biblical study to the purposes and practices of church life. The emphasis on the communal setting of interpretation springs from the goal of reconnecting the study of the Bible in the academy with the life and concerns of the church.

Another community-related goal of theological interpretation is to reconnect Christian scholars who have been separated from each other within the distinct disciplines of biblical studies and Christian theology. Each field has a traditionally established domain of discourse enforced by graduate school curricula, guild-based norms and practices, and the institutional drive toward specialization in modern bureaucratic society. Bringing biblical scholars and theologians together for the benefit of the church has many good effects. Directing scholarship toward the lived experiences of faith communities keeps it from becoming a closed loop defined by insider knowledge and self-referential discussions. Connecting biblical scholars and theologians can balance biblical scholarship's primary concern with history as the ultimate goal of study. It also invites theologians to step outside of a discourse defined primarily by philosophical categories and reengage with the unique logic and grammar of biblical texts that ground theological language in a living tradition and in concrete communities.

Canon

An emphasis on canon in theological interpretation speaks to the nature of the Bible as a fixed and limited collection of writings that has a normative function in the faith and practice of the church. The scope of the canon includes a fixed number of writings that are united with one another yet distinct from other writings. This sense of unity provides an invitation to relate the content of each text to the context of the whole. No matter how distinct a text is in content and message, it shares the status of being part of the canon with all other biblical texts. Theological interpretation emphasizes the canon as the ultimate literary context of a passage of Scripture.

The shape of the canon also plays an important role in theological interpretation. The major distinction within the biblical canon is the one between Old Testament and New Testament. Christian interpretation recognizes the Jewish Scriptures contained in the Christian Old Testament as a collection with its own integrity that existed and was acknowledged as authoritative Scripture prior to the origin of the church. Likewise, the New Testament has its own integrity, history of transmission, and internal narrative trajectory. Within each testament, the form of the biblical text as it exists within specific, distinct units or books functions as a guide to the understanding of the text within the communities that recognized them as bearing authoritative status. Nevertheless, the boundaries of the Christian canon indicate that both testaments contribute something necessary and distinct to the shape and content of the whole.

The exclusive character of the canon bears witness to the important function that these texts have served and continue to serve in believing communities. The canon functions as bearer of the authoritative tradition, as a source of communal identity, and as a guide to the worship, values, actions, and goals of the Christian community.

Critical Study

With all that has been said about the limitations of critical study for theological interpretation, one might think that theological interpretation would reject critical scholarship. This conclusion would be false. Theological interpretation acknowledges and celebrates the contributions of specially trained scholars whose work is essential to an informed reading of the Bible. The goal of theological interpretation is to integrate the results of critical study, when possible, into the church's understanding and use of the Bible for spiritual purposes. Theological interpretation sees critical study as a necessary yet insufficient element of biblical interpretation. As theologian Gabriel Fackre states, the guild of biblical scholarship cannot become a magisterium that determines the spiritual appropriation of Scripture by secular means.[43] Critical study cannot be neglected, but neither can it be the last word in interpretation.

One of the goals of critical study that theological interpretation does avoid is the attempt to "excavate" the text in order to reconstruct an earlier, and presumably more valuable, layer of meaning. Historical-critical study has valued earlier layers of the text to a greater degree because of the assumption that they lacked the supposedly value-laden, religiously motivated meaning of the final, canonical form. In reality, however, all layers of a text are value laden; otherwise the text would never have undergone the transformations that took place in the process of transmission. To privilege earlier layers as the aim of "history" and to treat later accretions as so much "debris" to be removed violate theological interpretation's emphasis on the church as the setting for interpretation and the canon as the definitive shape and form of the text.

Creed

Theological interpretation in a Christian context recognizes the continuity and mutuality between the content of the Bible and the summary statements of Christian belief expressed in ecumenical creeds. The church's ecumenical creeds provide brief narrative summaries of the Bible's chronologically and literarily diverse contents. The brevity and selectivity of the creeds make them incomplete witnesses to the full measure of revelation contained in the Bible. Statements such as the Apostles' Creed and the Nicene Creed say nothing about Israel and contain only the barest reference to the life of Jesus. They cannot replace the primary witness and authority of Scripture. Within these limitations, however, the creeds can serve as a reliable guide and a broad theological framework for evaluating individual texts in their relationship to one another within the broader context of the canon. Brief narratives summaries of faith provide a "rule of faith" to guide interpretation of varied texts within a sense of the Bible as a unified and coherent whole.

Theological interpretation of the Bible is the work of biblical scholars and theologians who bring their identities as committed Christian disciples to the task of interpreting Scripture. Although no specific methodology characterizes their work, the themes of communion, church, canon, critical study, and creed define the values that guide their interpretations of the Bible's meaning and message. Beyond these shared values, however, theological interpretation needs models for how to approach and carry out biblical study in comprehensive ways. I want to highlight two (among the many models that have been presented by previous studies) that address the primary goals and themes of theological interpretation. One model comes from a biblical scholar, the other from a systematic theologian. Together, they will provide a framework for the model of theological interpretation that I want to demonstrate through a study of Psalm 90.

MODELS OF THEOLOGICAL INTERPRETATION: BREVARD CHILDS AND GABRIEL FACKRE

Biblical scholars developed new approaches to biblical interpretation over the past forty years in response to the limitations of historical-critical studies. Many of these approaches drew on methodologies from the field of literary criticism in order to describe the ways that biblical texts worked as literary texts in their received form, as opposed to presumed earlier forms of the text that were the focus of historical criticism and literary source criticism. One development related to the newer literary study of the Bible was "canonical criticism," or "the canonical approach to Scripture." This approach focuses attention on the final form of biblical texts as they have been read in the setting of communities who revere it as sacred Scripture. This area of study is most often associated with the work of the late Brevard S. Childs, preeminent professor of Old Testament at Yale Divinity School.

Brevard Childs's Canonical Approach

Childs described his canonical approach to interpretation in his major works, *Introduction to the Old Testament as Scripture* and *Biblical Theology of the Old and New Testaments*.[44] A work that provides a concrete expression of his canonical approach to Scripture, however, is his commentary on the book of Exodus.[45] Childs's commentary broke the mold of the academic model of commentary writing in ways that continue to shape biblical scholarship to the present day. In it, he dealt with all of the traditional issues related to the critical study of Exodus as it had developed in the academy. These included issues such as identifying the best text, offering a fresh translation, and evaluating claims concerning the formation of the book in the earlier stages of oral transmission and in written form. These issues were standard items of academic commentary writing. After addressing these critical issues for each unit of text, however, Childs then addressed new elements of the text that were related to its form as canonical Scripture within living religious communities. After addressing the history of development "behind the text," Childs's focus was on the text as it stood in the context of the church's two-testament canon. He addressed the meaning of the text in the received form of the book of Exodus and in the larger context of the Old Testament. He added discussion of the text's influence on and reception in the New Testament wherever this was applicable. He also discussed the major elements of the text's interpretation by commentators and teachers who had received it as Scripture in Jewish and Christian history. The discussion of major moments in the history of interpretation often demonstrated how problems and tensions dealt with by critical scholars had been identified and resolved by ancient commentators in ways that were often as satisfactory as the results of modern critical study. Finally, he concluded his discussion of each literary unit with theological reflections on the text's contemporary implications for Christian theology in broad, ecumenical terms.

Childs's commentary provided a model of theological interpretation that has had a far-reaching influence on biblical studies, particularly study of the Old Testament. After Childs's commentary, subsequent commentators focused their work on the received form of the biblical text as opposed to reconstructed, earlier layers of the text to a much greater degree than before. Discussion of the history of interpretation, if only in the most cursory form, also began to appear with greater frequency in commentaries and exegetical essays, to the point of becoming a regular feature of many recent commentary series. Reflections on the implications of biblical texts for contemporary theology and religious and ethical practice also became a regular component of biblical commentaries after Childs.

Childs's Exodus commentary and his other writings on the significance of the canon for biblical interpretation have had a major influence on the theological interpretation of Scripture. Elements within the outline of his commentary address each of the major themes of theological interpretation discussed above: communion, church, canon, critical study, and creed. Childs's work began where many works of biblical interpretation begin, with a thorough critical exegesis of the text. The canonical setting of the text was obviously primary in his approach. Addressing the history of the text's interpretation in patristic, medieval, and Reformation sources located the text within the great tradition of the church. Theological reflection on the text provided an opportunity to highlight important intersections with the church's historic creeds or to address issues that the creeds pass over. In many ways, the canonical approach demonstrated in the outline of Childs's commentary provides a useful model for theological interpretation.

Gabriel Fackre's Pastoral Hermeneutics

Childs's commentary and writings on canonical interpretation of Scripture had a powerful influence on the second model of theological interpretation that I want to highlight. This model is found in the work of systematic theologian Gabriel Fackre. The second volume of his multivolume systematic theology addresses the doctrine of revelation, the authority of Scripture, and the challenges of biblical interpretation.[46] Fackre addressed his systematic theology specifically to Christian pastors in their work as stewards of the church's apostolic, priestly, and teaching office. He was familiar with the work and influence of Childs and incorporated Childs's contributions into his own exegetical approach. Fackre's work has the advantage of using the theological innovations that Childs introduced while also integrating Childs's model into a more systematic theological discussion of the role of the Bible in Christian faith and life.

Fackre's model of theological exegesis is based on what he described as the four senses of Scripture. He labeled these as the common sense, the critical sense, the canonical sense, and the contextual sense. His four senses of the text do not parallel the four senses of classical medieval exegesis. They do, however, intentionally draw on the ancient idea of affirming multiple levels of meaning as a necessary and preferable approach to biblical interpretation.

The Common Sense. The common sense is so named because it begins with the shared knowledge that most readers can agree on based on a general understanding of language, grammar, and the essential workings of literary texts. One major distinction is that Fackre defined the common sense of the text as the content of the text as it is understood by the Christian community in its shared life of worship and service.[47] For this community, and the pastors who serve it, the text is never less than Holy Scripture. Christians bring to the text their identity as members of a confessing and practicing community. The church's understanding of the text includes the ways that the church has been shaped to read and understand the text by prior tradition, including the history of interpretation it has inherited from previous generations. The focus of the common sense of the text is on what the text says to Christians in the context of their shared life as a faithful community of disciples.

Beginning with the church's understanding of the content of the text as Scripture differs from the pattern followed in Childs's commentary, which begins with the critical study of the text before moving into its canonical meaning. One reason that Childs began with the critical issues was because of the conventions of the genre of biblical commentary and his specific vocation as a biblical scholar. Beginning with the church's communal understanding of the content of the text grounds interpretation from the very beginning as a reading of the church's Bible studied as Scripture for churchly ends. It affirms the communal setting of interpretation in the church that is a hallmark of theological interpretation. The communal definition of the common sense of Scripture also emphasizes the pastor or teacher's location as a member of the community who reads the Bible in and with the church before taking on the specialized role of teaching and interpreting the Bible to the church and for the church. The common sense of Scripture stands within the Reformation tradition of the priesthood of all believers and the affirmation of the perspicuity of Scripture. Interpretation of the Bible for the church begins in the church and is done for the church's purposes of worship, proclamation, fellowship, and service.

The Critical Sense. While Fackre's pastoral hermeneutic does not begin with the critical study of the Bible, neither does it neglect or exclude it. Critical approaches to the Bible are authorized within Fackre's doctrine of revelation by the concept of general revelation. He describes this concept in narrative form by referring to the biblical covenant with Noah. The covenant with Noah describes a fallen humanity that nevertheless maintains some of the divine blessing bestowed in creation and is therefore capable of being addressed by and responding to divine revelation and inspired wisdom.[48] The theological understanding of human wisdom as fallen yet still bearing the image of God allows critical scholarship to be of value to the church. Critical scholarship can provide the church with perspectives that compensate for the church's own fallenness and its uncritical pursuit of its own interests and prejudices. Fackre was clearly aware of the tendencies toward naturalism and reductionism and the rejection of divine agency in critical scholarship. His doctrine of revelation, however, provided an understanding of the ways in which criticism, within proper limits, can serve as a corrective and as a catalyst to the church. Just as theological interpretation does not begin with critical methods, neither does it end with them. Critical study is necessary for the purposes and ends of the church, but it is not sufficient to achieve them.

The Canonical Sense. Childs's influence on biblical interpretation and on theology is clearly present in the third level of interpretation, which Fackre called the canonical sense. The canonical sense addresses the relationship between the individual text and the larger literary contexts of the book and testament in which it is found, and the broadest context of the canon as a whole.[49] These are the recontextualized settings that historical-critical scholarship tended to discount or intentionally sought to eliminate in its quest to arrive at the one, original, historical statement of "what the text meant." The canonical sense also takes into account the history of Christian interpretation preserved within the church's tradition. It is similar in function to "the rule of faith" in patristic exegesis. It provides a narrative theological framework in which the individual text can participate in the good news at the heart of the biblical story.

Several elements are important to the canonical sense of the text. One is the literary, intertextual connectivity between the text and the wider contexts of the Old and New Testaments. Literary connections within and between the Old and New Testaments are important as part of the church's two-testament Scripture. Another important element is the text's relationship to creedal statements of the church's ecumenical faith that provide outlines of the narrative arc of the biblical story. A third element is the tradition of interpretation in Christian history that provides examples of how the church has related the text to its confession of faith across various historical settings.

The Contextual Sense. The contextual sense of the text is its appropriation by the believing community for the specific aims of the church, typically described in the acts of worship, proclamation, fellowship, and ministry.[50] The church serves as the channel of communication between the revelation communicated in Scripture and the world that is the object of divine love and reconciliation. The text in its corporate dimension becomes a word "for us" and in its personal dimension becomes a word "for me." Fackre described multiple models of contextualization, including translation and paraphrase; transition/traduction (the analogical move from "then" to "now"); transformation of people, communities, and structures; and trajection, the forward tracking of implications that are suggested or initiated but not embodied in the biblical text.

THEOLOGICAL INTERPRETATION AS A SERIES OF FOUR IMPORTANT CONVERSATIONS

Fackre's four-fold model of interpretation seems on the surface to be a complex and demanding exercise. On one level, that is a true assessment. The central role of the Bible and the long and complicated history of its composition and interpretation require serious and careful work. On another level, however, it is possible to reframe Fackre's pastoral hermeneutic as a series of four important conversations about the meaning of a biblical text.

The first of these conversations, the common sense of the text, takes place within the local Christian community. The pastor/interpreter engages members of the local Christian fellowship in a conversation about the basic content, essential ideas, and general meaning of the text. The Bible is the church's book, and interpretation begins in the church. In this conversation, the minister gathers a community of disciples around the biblical text to read and to listen to it as a word that addresses the community as the people of God. The minister bears the identity of a Christian who reads the text as a participant in the ministry of the church and in the worship and service of God.

The second conversation about the critical sense of the text is with biblical scholars whose work takes place primarily in the academy. The minister engages in this conversation as an educated person who has acquired the skills and knowledge needed to gain access to the information about the texts made available by experts in the study of biblical literature. In this conversation, both the minister and the guild of scholars bear the theological identity of finite and fallen human beings who nevertheless still bear the lingering blessing and image of God. The image of God makes them capable of knowing and responding to the divine word of revelation. In this conversation, the general revelation available to all can broaden the perspective of the church beyond the narrow interests of its common sense interpretation.

The conversation with academic scholarship in the critical sense of the text is a necessary but insufficient conversation, however. In the canonical sense, the minister enters into conversation with Christian theologians who are heirs of the Scripture in its canonical shape and who interpret the Old and New Testaments under a rule of faith that has shaped the reading of Scripture from earliest times. The canon, the creeds, and the chorus of interpreters from across the scope of Christian history are essential conversation partners in interpretation of Scripture. Finally, in the contextual sense of the text, the minister enters into conversation with the world outside of the church. She reads Scripture as one called to lead the church as it shares what it has received with the world that is both beyond the church and also within the church, a world in need of hope and redemption.

Fackre's model of theological interpretation has many strengths. It incorporates all of the elements of theological interpretation that are characteristic of this recent movement. It is the result of a thoughtful doctrine of revelation that unfolds from the key moments of the biblical narrative. It is pastoral in aim, focusing on the office within the church tasked with leading forward the church's apostolic mission. In its four movements, it seeks to integrate the disciplines of biblical studies, systematic theology, and church history. It is thoroughly church-centered, beginning the task of interpretation in the context of Christian community yet not neglecting the church's call to exercise its mission in the world.

The method is not without some limitations, however. It is a demanding assignment. It essentially requires the pastor to do the kind of integrative work that the biblical scholar, systematic theologian, and church historian are not required to do by virtue of their disciplinary specialization. It is potentially an overly intellectual process, though only if the contextual sense results in statements without actions or virtues. Skeptics might ask whether all four conversations are necessary. Why could one not move from the common sense straight to contextualization, or focus on either the critical or canonical sense alone? Neglect of critical study, however, ignores the theological truth that the church is as fallen and in need of redemption as the world is. Ignoring the canonical sense, on the other hand, would result in a process that brings contemporary culture into the church through the door of critical study, but without providing a doorway through which the .revelatory word can enter into the culture.

In summary, Fackre's model is a promising, theologically grounded framework for carrying out the goals of theological interpretation. It neither neglects nor yields the floor entirely to critical scholarship. Instead, it provides a model for integrating both religious and critical approaches to reading Scripture within a comprehensive plan. As promising as Fackre's model is, it is surprising that there is little evidence in print that his model has been applied to the interpretation of biblical texts for the purposes of Christian ministry. The most likely reason for this is the strict disciplinary boundaries that were still entrenched between biblical studies and theology at the time that Fackre proposed his hermeneutic. As the discussion on the theological interpretation of Scripture has suggested, those boundaries have become significantly less important in the past two decades. Now is an opportune time to demonstrate the benefits of Fackre's model for theological interpretation. The remainder of this book applies this model to the interpretation of Psalm 90 with the goal of exploring further how to gain a heart of wisdom by a more comprehensive reading of this text. By showing the benefits of this model for Psalm 90, I also hope to demonstrate the promise of the model for theological interpretation of other biblical texts as well. It is to this goal that we now turn.

Chapter 3

The Common Sense of the Text: A Conversation with the Church

Theological interpretation of Scripture seeks to bring the resources of biblical scholarship and Christian theology together to help Christians read the Bible in ways that reflect the character of God, who addresses us in Scripture. The recent emphasis on theological interpretation has resulted in part from an acknowledgment that critical biblical scholarship's focus on a single meaning, based on historical reconstruction and isolated from the communities that preserve and transmit the Bible as Scripture, is not sufficient to sustain the purposes of the church. It also acknowledges a detrimental divide between the work of Christian theologians and the task of careful interpretation of biblical texts. Key emphases of theological interpretation of Scripture include understanding Scripture as a vehicle for communion with God, the shared life of the church as the primary context of interpretation, the harmonious testimony of the church's two-testament canon, the guiding framework of ancient ecumenical creeds, the relevance of premodern interpretation, the integration of critical inquiry and confessional reading, and the contextualization of Scripture in the setting of the contemporary world.

Though many models of theological interpretation have been used in the past two decades, I want to demonstrate the benefits of a model set forth by theologian Gabriel Fackre in his pastoral systematic theology.[51] Fackre proposed a four-fold approach to theological interpretation that acknowledges multiple levels of meaning within the biblical text, locates the interpretation of the Bible in the active life of the church, integrates the results of critical study with the life of faith, and grounds biblical interpretation in a coherent Christian doctrine of revelation.

The beginning point for Christian theological exegesis is what Fackre labels the common sense of the text. The term has clear parallels with the ancient Jewish and Christian references to the "plain sense" or the literal sense of the text. An emphasis on the common sense of the text does not exclude other levels of meaning. It is, however, the beginning point for interpretation.

Fackre's description of the common sense has two important components. First, as the name implies, it focuses on the content of the text as an ordinary use of language that is accessible to anyone with a basic understanding of vocabulary, grammar, rhetoric, and the workings of literary texts. The common sense of the text is based on the level of access to textual meaning shared in common by all readers or hearers. The second component, however, sets Fackre's description apart from a kind of survey of the text that could be applied to any work of literature. He restricts the common sense of Scripture to information about the text that is available to the Christian community that reads it together as a worshiping body committed to serving the God revealed in Israel and Jesus. The restriction of the common sense to the Christian community is an acknowledgment that the Christian Bible originated in the church and took shape as Holy Scripture for the purposes of Christian devotion. Therefore, the beginning point for interpretation is in the community that preserves, reveres, and lives out the Bible as inspired Scripture. The starting point in a theological interpretation of Scripture is to engage in a conversation with members of the church about the church's own Bible.

This point may seem obvious and unnecessary. Some might object that the literary content of the Bible is the same for readers within and outside of the church. It is true that in the long period of Constantinian Christianity from the fourth century onward, when the church's interpretation of the Bible enjoyed broad cultural and political authority in the West, critical scholarship could take the church's interpretation for granted and could offer its own historically grounded and critically informed interpretation of the Bible as an alternative. Critical scholarship originated in a cultural context dominated by the church's interpretation of the biblical narrative as the normative understanding of the natural and moral universe. Academic scholarship has long been influenced by a need to create an intellectual and institutional space for free inquiry independent of the established church's teaching. Much of the history of Western secularization can be defended as necessary and beneficial. Regardless of one's view of the positive or negative effects of secularization, however, the key point for this discussion is that secularization has progressed to such a degree that knowledge of the content and overarching narrative of the Bible is no longer a widely held or supported part of popular culture or consciousness. Academic biblical scholarship in past generations could choose to begin interpretation with a critical approach to the text because it could assume the confessional stance of the church as a given and take the leading position of the church in the culture for granted. The period of the dominance of historical criticism was also a period in which knowledge of the church's traditional approach to the Bible could be widely assumed within the culture, particularly among segments of the culture that had access to higher education. Over the course of the latter half of the twentieth century, however, the nominal Christian influence that was once dispersed throughout culture as a whole gave way to a post-Christian, secular culture.[52] Biblical interpreters and commentators can no longer assume familiarity with the broad biblical narrative or the general content of the Bible, much less a Christian interpretation of the Bible's primary narrative. To begin interpretation with a critical approach, as is the typical approach of academic study of the Bible, is to disabuse most readers of ideas about the Bible that they never acquired to begin with. The question for initial interpretation is no longer, "What do I need to know about the text that I cannot learn from the church's interpretation alone?" The necessary initial question is, "What is in this text, and what does it say to the Christian community?"

Though biblical knowledge within the church is seemingly at an ebb tide in contemporary Western culture, the church still possesses a shared body of knowledge about the Bible and a shared understanding of its content. The common sense of Scripture also includes not only the members of the local body gathered for teaching or worship but also the broad tradition of the church that is spread across the globe and the deep biblical understanding of the communion of saints across Christian history. The meaning of the text as shared among Christians in the local and global church, present and past, is part of the common sense of the text.

Many guides and instructional manuals for both the reading of literature in general and for biblical exegesis in particular suggest that readers begin with an introductory survey of the basic content and "terrain" of the text. A recent, popular introduction to biblical interpretation, Michael Gorman's *Elements of Biblical Exegesis*, labels the first necessary element in the process of exegesis as the element of "Survey."[53] A survey of the text is an initial reading to gain awareness of the content, shape, and primary ideas contained within it. The common sense of the text in Fackre's model is similar to Gorman's first element of Survey, with the important exception that the reader embraces the specific identity of a committed Christian disciple who surveys the text in the context of Christian community, defined locally as a specific congregation and globally as the communion of saints living and dead. The common sense of Scripture is identified by people who read the text as Christians among Christians.

READING IN TRANSLATION

Since the common sense of the text takes the perspective of the Christian community as a whole, it uses modern translations in the language of the church's worship and study. English-speaking Christians have a wide array of translations from which to choose. The most important distinction among translations is between formal equivalence and functional equivalence.[54] Formal equivalence translations attempt to represent the structure and wording of the original language as closely as possible while achieving a smooth and readable text in the target language. The functional equivalence approach aims to produce a translation that reflects current English language usage that is clear and readable by expressing the equivalent meaning of the original text but not necessarily the original wording and structure. Functional equivalence translations tend to make specific translational choices in the target language from among a range of possible meanings in the wording of the original language. Formal equivalence translations in general tend to leave decisions about the possible meanings of broad or vague language in the hands of the reader of the translation rather than selecting one specific meaning out of the range of options allowed by the wording of the original text. For the purpose of understanding the meaning of biblical texts, it is best to begin with formal equivalence translations before moving to functional equivalence translations.

Psalm 90 provides a good example of the differences between formal equivalence and functional equivalence translations and their use in v. 11. The King James Version (KJV) reads, "Who knoweth the power of thine anger? Even according to thy fear, so is thy wrath." This is a literal translation of the original language that represents its wording and order very closely. The meaning of the original language of the second half of the verse, however, is unclear in both the Hebrew text and in the KJV. The Hebrew text describes some correspondence between God's fear and God's wrath. It is unclear, however, how these two concepts are related. Although grammatically the words "thy fear" can be understood either as the fear people have toward God or the fear that God has, there are no biblical texts that make God the subject of the verb "to fear." The term is universally understood as the state of fear that people express toward God. To further complicate matters, the "fear of God" in biblical language is an idiom, a figure of speech that means something other than the literal wording of the phrase. The English phrase "raining cats and dogs" has little to do with the literal wording of the phrase. It is an idiom for a very heavy downpour. The biblical idiom "fear of God" means something like "the response of reverent awe and submission appropriate to the presence of God." It can refer to proper religious and ethical behavior or to the kind of life that should result from an awareness of the presence of God. The KJV does not explain the idiom but rather represents the wording of the original. This is intentional on the part of the translators. It leaves the question of interpretation to the reader of the translation rather than narrowing the range of interpretations in the translation.

Interestingly, the New International Version (NIV), the New American Standard Bible (NASB), and the New Revised Standard Version (NRSV) all go a step further toward interpretation of the phrase "thy fear" than does the KJV. They translate "thy fear" as "the fear that is due you." This is the most widely accepted understanding of the concept of "the fear of God," and the translations make this understanding explicit in English. Some of the translations also clarify the most difficult question raised by the wording of v. 11. How does the wrath of God, that is, the sense of displeasure God expresses toward humanity, correspond to the reverence that humans express toward God? The NIV and NRSV provide one possible answer. They both translate the end of v. 11 in a similar way: NIV, "Your wrath is as great as the fear that is your due," and NRSV, "Your wrath is as great as the fear that is due you." In other words, God's wrath corresponds to the fear that humans should rightfully express toward God. Refusal to acknowledge God appropriately provokes a proportional response from God. This is one possible meaning of the unclear wording of the original language. Two popular functional equivalence translations, the Contemporary English Version (CEV) and the New Living Translation (NLT), provide a similar translation. Other explanations are possible, however, as shown by the Good News Translation (GNT) and The Message (MSG).

The GNT translates the second half of v. 11 as "Who knows what fear your fury can bring?" In this translation, the question in the first half of the verse, "Who knows the power of your anger?" is carried over to the second half, and the fear of God is interpreted as a result of divine wrath.

God's wrath provokes human fear. The Message offers another interpretation. "Who can make sense of such rage, such anger against the very ones who fear you?" In this interpretation, the wrath of God falls on those who express the proper fear of God. This translation reads v. 11 as a complaint that God's wrath is not diminished by the piety of those who experience it. This is yet another possible interpretation of the vague wording of v. 11 in the original language.

Psalm 90:11 illustrates the differences between formal equivalence and functional equivalence translations and their differing roles in interpretation. A formal equivalence translation preserves the wording of the original in clear English, and if the original is vague or general in meaning, the translation leaves the interpretation to the reader to investigate and to clarify. In Psalm 90:11 specifically, the KJV best fulfills the goals of a formal equivalence translation. Functional equivalence translations, on the other hand, attempt to make the meaning of the original as clear as possible in English, even if that involves choosing one possible interpretation and making it part of the translation itself. The fact that formal equivalence translations like the NIV, NASB, and NRSV clarify the translation of Psalm 90:11 given by the KJV is likely due to their historical dependence on the KJV and a desire to improve on the clarity of the KJV while following the template it established. The translations of GNT and MSG are the most specific about the English meaning. However, they do this by choosing for the reader one interpretation out of the possible meanings of the original text. Since addressing the common sense of the text is the beginning point of theological interpretation rather than the end point, it is best to use formal equivalence translations that allow the reader the widest range of options and leave the use of functional equivalence translation to a later stage of the process.

ELEMENTS OF PSALM 90 FAMILIAR TO THE CHRISTIAN COMMUNITY

The common sense of the text is a beginning point for interpretation, not the end of the interpretation process. Therefore, it is not necessary to address all questions presented by the text in detail. Members of the worshiping community who read the psalm for personal devotion, communal worship, and as a means of greater communion with God and others do not need to address all points of interpretation for these purposes in the same level of detail as those who hold the teaching and preaching offices of the church or who are equipped for the specialized work of scholarship. The common sense, however, is the place where these various groups within the church and the community meet and where interpretation begins. The primary question of the common sense of the text is "What does it say?" Answering this question involves first paying attention to elements of the text that are familiar to able readers and committed members of the Christian community. Psalm 90 contains several elements that serve as helpful examples.

The Context of the Psalms

Christian readers identify the book of Psalms as a collection of prayers and hymns from the people of Israel that have been taken up by the church as part of its literature for worship, devotion, and doctrinal teaching. They associate the psalms in general with the figure of King David due to the large number of psalms that are ascribed to David or that mention David in their titles. Most Christians are familiar with selected psalms that are used on frequent occasions such as funerals, or with selected lines of certain psalms that are used regularly as liturgical elements such as a call to worship or a prayer of confession or a litany of praise. The psalms are most often used as liturgical resources for corporate worship, as guides to private prayer, as the basis for religious hymnody and songs, and as texts of consolation and encouragement in times of crisis. Psalms such as 23, 46, or 91 are frequently used devotionally or for meditation in times of crisis or stress. Psalm 51 is often used for corporate and personal confession of sin. Psalm 90, with its reflection on the eternal nature of God and the brevity of human life, has often served as a Scripture reading for Christian funerals. It is also known through Isaac Watts's popular paraphrase in the hymn "O God, Our Help in Ages Past."

The Title: "A Prayer of Moses, the Man of God"

The title of Psalm 90 provides a sense of both orientation and disorientation for Christian readers. The title of the psalm as a prayer is certainly in keeping with the primary expectation and use of the psalms in Christian experience and with the content of the psalm overall. The ascription of the psalm to Moses, one of the major figures of the Bible, gives it a connection to the central narrative of the Old Testament, Israel's exodus from Egypt. The exodus event also includes Israel's covenant with God at Mt. Sinai and their long journey through the wilderness toward the promised land. Moses is the central figure in this narrative and in Israel's religious heritage overall. The title of the psalm gives the Christian imagination much space for reflection in connecting the psalm to the narrative of Moses' life and his role in redemptive history. The outline of Moses' career, from his dramatic call at the burning bush to his confrontation with the king of Egypt, his role in the deliverance of Israel at the sea, his unique status as the lawgiver and mediator of Israel's covenant, and his leadership during the long sojourn in the wilderness are all familiar elements of the exodus narrative. Moses was the consummate religious leader of ancient Israel. A prayer ascribed to him provides a broad narrative range for imagining the kind of life experiences that inform such a prayer.

The name of Moses, however, is also a somewhat disorienting sign for both critical and confessional readers of Psalm 90, though for different reasons. The ascription of a psalm, and indeed any biblical writing, to Moses is met with great skepticism if not universal rejection on the part of many critical scholars. Most consider Moses to be a legendary figure from Israel's lore regarding their earliest times. Though the narratives about Moses may be traced back to some specific historical circumstances, critical scholarship considers the likelihood of written material being composed and passed down from a figure of such antiquity to be highly doubtful. Moses is treated in scholarship less as an author than as an authority figure that grants a sense of antiquity and legitimacy to the collected religious traditions of ancient Israel.

Confessional Christian readers, on the other hand, pause at the mention of Moses in Psalm 90 for different reasons. Christian worshipers tend to take biblical titles either at face value or at least as reliable, functional guides for reading. The mention of Moses is disjunctive not because they are prone to question any association between him and the biblical text but rather because the primary authoritative and authorizing figure in the Psalms is not Moses but David. Evidence of hesitation about the Mosaic nature of the psalm can already be seen in some manuscripts of the Greek translation of Psalm 90 where the title is not "the prayer *of* Moses," using an article in the possessive case, but rather "the prayer *concerning* Moses." The strong association of the Psalms with David appears in Augustine's commentary on Psalm 90.[55] Augustine labeled the phrase "the prayer of Moses, the man of God," as a title, indicating that the psalm is in some way related to Moses but nevertheless should be attributed to David as were most of the other untitled psalms.

The title "the prayer of Moses" in a book focused primarily on David gives the impression that the psalm is distinct from other prayers in the Psalms, an impression that is borne out in its content as well. Consideration of the psalm in its immediate literary context underscores its distinctiveness from the surrounding material. Psalm 89 ends with a bitter communal lament over the fall of the kingdom of David. In addition to Psalm 90, most of the other references to Moses in Psalms are found in Psalms 90–106. As I will discuss when I take up the topic of the critical and canonical senses of the text, Psalm 90's association with Moses provides a different point of view than the many psalms referring to David in the Psalms.

The title of Psalm 90 as a prayer is in keeping with the expectations of the book of Psalms as a whole and with the content of the psalm itself, which is addressed in its entirety to God in the second person singular. Prayer is a fundamental action of Christian devotion. A prayer ascribed to or associated with the leading religious authority of the Christian Old Testament is an important and formative model of prayer.

One element of Psalm 90 that relates to the title "The Prayer of Moses" is the specific form of prayer that it represents. Psalm 90 is a prayer of the community as a whole. Within the prayers of the book of Psalms, Psalm 90 stands alongside the prayers prayed by the entire worshiping community such as Psalms 44, 56, 74, and 89. These prayers address God collectively, using the first person plural pronouns *we, us,* and *our.* From first to last, Psalm 90 is voiced as a prayer of the people as a whole. "Lord, you have been *our* dwelling place in all generations" (v. 1); " *We* are consumed by your anger" (v. 7); "So teach *us* to count *our* days that *we* may gain a wise heart" (v. 12); "Let the favor of the Lord *our* God be upon *us,* and prosper for *us* the work of *our* hands" (v. 17; emphasis added).[56]

The communal form of the prayer raises questions about the relationship between the prayer and the title "a prayer of Moses." Is the primary speaking voice the voice of an individual like Moses who speaks for the community as a whole? Christians are familiar with this form of communal prayer in the pastoral prayers of Christian worship in which an individual minister prays on behalf of the congregation as a whole. Alternately, the title could connote a prayer originating from an individual leader that is to be voiced by the community as a whole. The Lord's Prayer, which begins with "Our Father," is the best-known Christian example of such a prayer. In either case, Christians are familiar with prayers prayed by an individual that are voiced by the worshiping community as a whole. Psalm 90 is such a prayer. The individual pray-er prays Psalm 90 as a member of a congregation at worship.

Praise of God in Time and Eternity

Verses 1-2 introduce a key theme of the psalm and a major attribute of God used across the narrative scope of the Bible. God is the eternal dwelling place of the worshiping community. Verse 1 praises God as the constant dwelling place of God's people in all generations, while v. 2 praises God's eternal existence beyond time as the creator of the world. Verse 2 expresses this central conviction about God in language that is both poetic and mythological in nature. It describes creation as a process of God giving birth to the world. The NASB translation, which describes itself as one of the most literal English translations, conveys this sense of the original language in v. 2: "Before the mountains were born, or you gave birth to the earth and the world . . . . You are God." While the mythological imagery is in tension with the description of creation by divine command in Genesis 1 and with the general Christian rejection of mythological language for creation, such imagery gives the psalm an impression of arising from a distant past, a time in which such language was the common way of describing creation. It therefore contributes to an impression of antiquity consistent with an ancient figure like Moses.

God's timeless nature and character are conveyed in the choice of wording at the conclusion of v. 2: "From everlasting to everlasting, you are God." The direct address to God in the present tense affirms the eternal being of God. In all times and before all times, God is God. This theme is familiar to the Christian community not only through its reading of Scripture but also through its worship and hymnody, its creedal statements, and its confessions of faith.

Verses 1-2 open the psalm on a note of praise for God as the dwelling place of God's people and the eternal ruler over all creation. Such praise is often the beginning point of Christian worship. God's faithfulness, holiness, and sovereignty draw forth the praise and confidence of the people who have learned to call on "the Lord."

The Brevity of Human Life

The second unit of the psalm, vv. 3-6, shifts to a different topic: the qualitative difference between the eternal God and transient human beings. Viewed in the light of God's eternal nature, human life is exceedingly fragile and fleeting. The psalm traces the brevity of human life to a declaration given by God: "You turn us back to dust, and say, 'Turn back, you mortals'" (v. 3). This declaration is somewhat vague, but Christian readers can hear echoes of the creation narrative in Genesis 2. There God formed the first human from the dust of the ground. Verse 3 also echoes the judgment scene of Genesis 3 where, after the first man and woman had eaten from the forbidden fruit of the tree of the knowledge of good and evil, they were punished with pain and struggle "until you return to the ground from which you were taken, for you are dust, and to dust you shall return" (Gen 3:19 NABRE). The American Standard Version and the New Jewish Publication Society translate the word for "dust" in v. 3 with the English word "destruction," indicating that Psalm 90 uses a different Hebrew word here than the word for dust in Genesis 2–3. Conceptually, however, the idea is generally the same in both contexts. Humanity is defined by limits of mortality set by God.

Following v. 3, the psalm offers a montage of images to describe the brevity of human life. A thousand years in God's sight are like a single yesterday when it is past, like a three-hour watch in the dark of night, like a dream after awakening, and like the desert grass that flourishes with the morning dew only to wither in the heat of the day. If even a lengthy time span such as a thousand years is a brief moment in God's perspective, then the brief span of a human life is like nothing at all. Against the ongoing flow of divine life, a human life span is almost imperceptible.

Psalm 90's emphasis on the brevity of human life before God has made it a frequent text for Christian funerals. In times of grief, it underscores the finitude and fragility of each human life. The psalm's allusion to "returning to dust" locates the reality of death within the larger biblical narrative of God's limitations on human autonomy and on death as a result of human alienation from God. The next section of the psalm makes the connection between death and judgment explicit.

Consumed by God's Wrath

Verses 3-6 assign the responsibility for the brevity of human life to God. God turns humankind back to dust. Verses 7-10 introduce a new element into this picture: the theme of God's wrath in response to human sin. Verses 7-8 read, "For we are consumed by your anger; by your wrath we are overwhelmed. You have set our iniquities before you, our secret sins in the light of your countenance." The light of God's presence exposes human fallibility. God's wrath compounds the brevity of life with troubles. This description also echoes themes from Genesis 1–11. In Genesis 3, the woman was assigned pain in childbirth and the man was given over to toil and strain in labor as a result of breaking God's command not to eat from the tree in the midst of the garden. They were expelled from the garden of delight and from access to the tree of life. In Genesis 6, just prior to the decree to destroy the earth with a flood, God declared a limit to human life span (Gen 6:3). Genesis 6:5 explains, "The LORD saw the wickedness of humankind was great in the earth, and that every inclination of the thoughts of their hearts was only evil continually." Psalm 90 laments circumstances that are similar to the judgments that Genesis 3 and 6 narrate. Divine wrath places a limit on the number and quality of human years. Though a person's life may extend to seventy or even eighty years, these are beset with toil and trouble and come to an end like a sigh.

The negative view of human nature and human life portrayed in vv. 7-10 is not unique in the Old Testament, but it is in contrast with another view in the Old Testament that affirms and celebrates the goodness of human life. Genesis 1 affirms humanity as the crowning act of creation. Humans alone among creation are said to bear the image of God (Gen 1:26-28). This view is affirmed in Psalm 8, where humanity is praised as "a little lower than God, and crowned . . . with glory and honor" (v. 5). The understanding of the world and humanity as creations of the redeeming God of Israel gives much of the Old Testament a world-affirming and life-affirming character. One place where the pessimistic view of life prevails, however, is in the book of Ecclesiastes. Ecclesiastes declares repeatedly that the finality of death cancels out any momentary gains made in life: "What do mortals get from all the toil and strain with which they toil under the sun? For all their days are full of pain, and their work is a vexation; even at night their minds do not rest. This also is vanity" (2:22-23).

The view expressed in Psalm 90 that human life is lived under the wrath of God appears in the New Testament in Paul's letter to the Romans. In chapters 1–3, Paul argues that all people, both Jew and Gentile alike, live out their lives under the wrath of God as a result of their refusal to acknowledge God's sole claim to sovereignty or to live out the full extent of righteousness instructed in the Law. Though Paul does not cite Psalm 90 in support of his argument, his description of the human condition is similar to the effect of the wrath of God described in vv. 7-10.

From Wrath to Wisdom

The contrast between the eternal God and finite human beings seen in the first ten verses of Psalm 90 leads to a question and a request in vv.

11-12: "Who considers [Heb., "knows"] the power of your anger? . . . So teach us to count our days that we may gain a wise heart." The question, "Who knows?" often implies a negative answer in the Old Testament (cf. Eccl 3:21). "Who knows the power of your wrath," however, is an ambiguous question. Verses 7-10 have just declared that the power of God's wrath consumes all the years of human life. In this light, everyone should know the power of God's wrath. The NRSV translation addresses this tension between vv. 7-10 and v. 11 by identifying the issue as one of understanding rather than knowledge. It reads, "Who considers the power of your anger?" The suggestion is that most people do not fully understand the truth that is declared in vv. 7-10, namely, that God's power to limit and judge human iniquity outstrips all efforts to circumvent it.

As described above, the second line of v. 11 is difficult to understand. The words are easy to translate, as the literal translation of KJV demonstrates: "Even according to thy fear, so is thy wrath." Yet the meaning of the comparison between the fear of God and the wrath of God is unclear. A clearer understanding of v. 11b must wait until discussion of the critical sense of the text. Regardless of the meaning of v. 11b, however, v. 12 offers a request for what is lacking in v. 11. Verse 11 asks, "Who knows?" Verse 12 requests, "So teach us to count our days that we may gain a wise heart." The knowledge that would lead to wisdom is the knowledge of how "to count our days." What appears to be lacking is a genuine grasp of the situation described in vv. 3-10, the brevity of life lived under divine wrath. Human life is restricted by the power of divine wrath, yet, to paraphrase v. 11, "who truly perceives or considers the power of your [God's] wrath?" The presumed answer is, "No one." The apparent meaning, the common-sense meaning, of v. 12 is that if God were to give people the understanding to count their finite number of days, they would gain the wisdom to live rightly.

In Psalm 90, the wrath of God has both a limiting and a punitive purpose. The manifestation of God's wrath against the condition of sin is the limiting of the human lifespan. This judgment limits the damage that humans can inflict upon themselves and upon God's world through their autonomy and rejection of divine rule. Psalm 90 also suggests that wrath may have a corrective purpose as well. Following the NRSV and NIV translations of v. 11, the psalm describes a correspondence between the wrath of God and the proper fear or reverence that people ought to express. Knowledge of the brevity of life, which is the main effect of God's wrath, would lead to a proper reverence for God and to genuine wisdom. Since people cannot seem to recognize this on their own ("Who knows?"), the psalm prays for divine help and intervention. Psalm 90 describes the path to wisdom as one that leads to an understanding of the human condition from the perspective of biblical narratives like the ones that are recorded in Genesis 1–11.

Prayers for Mercy and Grace

Verses 1-12 praise God's unceasing faithfulness and eternal nature, lament humanity's brief and troubled existence, and confess the wrongs that cast the shadow of divine judgment on human life. These verses conclude with a prayer for help to recognize the true nature of the human condition in relation to God and to gain wisdom to respond appropriately. The prayer of v. 12 could be an appropriate conclusion to the psalm, but it is not. Verses 13-17 add a series of additional requests on behalf of the worshiping community.

Verse 13 calls out to God using the covenant name of the LORD, Yahweh, and asks for the LORD to "turn" from a disposition of wrath to one of compassion. The request is not on behalf of humanity as a whole, however, as seems to be the case in vv. 1-12 (v. 3, "Turn back, you mortals"), but rather is voiced on behalf of "your servants," the servants of Yahweh, the covenant people of God. Verse 14 contains a petition for the steadfast love that defines the essence of the relationship between God and God's people. This term is translated in a variety of ways in the Old Testament, including loving kindness, tender mercies, and faithfulness. Each of these translations captures an element of the fundamental quality that preserves the covenantal relationship between God and Israel. Verse 16 prays both for God's servants and also for their children, asking that they be allowed to see the work and glory of God. The psalm concludes with a plaintive request that God establish the work of the people's hands. Since this prayer is voiced by God's servants, the work of their hands includes their work done in service to God. Though the prayer previously complained that human life is exceedingly brief and full of trouble, it ends with a desire that the community's work for God might be of lasting value. In sum, the psalm concludes its description of human life lived under the divine wrath with a prayer that God will turn the tide, as it were, through some act of compassion and mercy that would restore God's people from affliction to joy and from futility to fruitfulness.

Verses 1-12 offer a description of human life in the pattern of Genesis 1–11, a life constrained by the effects of human sinfulness. Verses 13-17, on the other hand, offer a prayer suited to the narrative of the book of Exodus. The closest parallel to these verses is in the prayer of Moses on behalf of the people of Israel in the context of the golden calf episode in Exodus 32. While Moses is alone on the mountain awaiting God's instructions for the people, God reports to him that the people at the foot of the mountain have turned away to revel in idolatry. Upon hearing God's intention to bring total judgment on the people of Israel and to begin anew with Moses alone, Moses ignores God's instruction to leave God alone and responds instead with an urgent intercession for mercy that includes the words "turn . . . and relent" (Exod 32:12 ESV), the same words that appear in Psalm 90:13. These words in v. 13 provide the closest link between Psalm 90 and a prayer of Moses recorded elsewhere in the Bible, and they may indeed be the inspiration for the title of the psalm, "the prayer of Moses." The "prayer of Moses" is fundamentally a prayer for God to turn away from the wrath of judgment and to turn back toward God's servants with grace and favor.

Christians who read and pray Psalm 90 have learned to see themselves as part of the servants of the Lord who have received mercy and grace and who want to see the work of the Lord revealed and established. This understanding, sadly, has a dark side in the long history of Christians claiming for themselves the promises to Israel, while describing the people of Israel as rejected and cut off from God. This kind of self-serving interpretation has done little to help the church since it has often led to a form of counterfeit righteousness that is based on the rejection of Israel and the Jewish people rather than genuine faithfulness on the part of the church. While the idea that the church has superseded the Jewish people as heirs of the covenant has been detrimental to the church, it has been tragic and deadly to the Jews, resulting in prejudice, discrimination, and persecution time and time again in places where the Christian church held sway or sought favor with the power of the state. It is far better for Christians to see themselves as having been graciously included into God's enduring covenant with Israel, whose gracious origins and divine mission are at the heart of this prayer. In Psalm 90, Israel prays as a part of humanity living under the wrath of God, and also as people who have received enough mercy from God in the past to ask boldly for mercy again so that God's work and glory may be revealed in new and greater ways.

A Christian reading of Psalm 90 recognizes the answer to the petition in v. 13 for God to turn back toward God's servants with compassion to have been answered in the life of Jesus.[57] In the redemptive work of Christ, Christians receive inclusion in the life and mission of God's servants who are the beneficiaries of the petitions of this prayer. As people who have received the requests of vv. 13-15 for compassion, love, and joy, they may also pray the petitions of vv. 16 and 17 that they and their children may see the work and glory of God fully revealed, and that their own work for God may be firmly established. A Christian interpretation of vv. 13-17, therefore, has the "already, but not yet" dimension shared in many Old Testament texts that are read as promises for the Christian community. The petitions for God's mercy are seen as answered in the gracious appearing of Jesus as God's anointed. At the same time, the desire for the glory of the Lord to be revealed to God's servants and their children and for the work of God's servants to be established points toward a future hope that still awaits fulfillment.

CONCLUSION: THE UNFAMILIAR FEATURES OF PSALM 90

Psalm 90 presents a familiar setting for Christian readers: the corporate worship and prayer of the people of God. Such worship acknowledges God as the sovereign and eternal creator of life and as the true sanctuary for God's people in all generations. In a setting of genuine worship, the eternal nature of God exposes the fragile and fleeting nature of human life. This distinction is made stronger by God's wrathful response to human presumptions of autonomy, including both the blatant wrongs and the secret rebellions that are revealed in the light of God's presence. In the view of this prayer, the power of God's wrath overwhelms any efforts at a fruitful life apart from God. Only an inspired awareness of the human condition in relation to God can yield the power to live wisely.

In the context of worship and a consideration of the human condition that is informed by Israel's Scriptures, the quest to understand the request that God "teach us to count our days that we may gain a wise heart" has its initial answer. Who rightly considers the brevity of life in light of God's eternal nature and purpose? We need guidance to "count our days" properly in the context of our relationship with God. To learn to maximize the time we are allotted, day by day, is the path to a wise heart.

Psalm 90 goes beyond the request for wisdom to make the most of the limited span of life, however. It boldly asks for God to change God's disposition from wrath to compassion and mercy. This boldness follows the model of Moses' intercession for Israel during the episode with the golden calf and seeks the same fidelity of God that established the covenant relationship with Israel in days of old. Christians can identify with the universal condition of rebellion and wrath of vv. 3-12 and with the special favor of God that invites the prayer for mercy in vv. 13-17. They see the prayer for God to "turn . . . [and] have compassion" answered in the ministry of Jesus, and see themselves as the beneficiaries of God's extension of Israel's covenant through faith in the work of God revealed in Christ.

Christian readers have a framework for understanding the message of Psalm 90 as a result of their practice of worship, their reading of the broad narrative sweep of Scripture, and the church's tradition of understanding the Christ event through the language and lens of the Old Testament. Not all elements of Psalm 90, however, can be clearly grasped from a common Christian reading alone. For all the parts of Psalm 90 that seem familiar, there are other elements that evade a surface reading.

For example, the identity of God as Creator in v. 2 is familiar to Christian understanding, but the imagery of God giving birth to the mountains and the earth is not. The awareness of the brevity and difficulty of life is a familiar concept, but the negative portrayal of long life as only "toil and trouble" is more pessimistic than other portrayals of human existence in both the Old Testament and the New Testament. The relationship between the fear of God and the wrath of God in v. 11 is expressed in vague terms and is hard to understand in its present form. Is it possible to clarify what this proposed correspondence between fear and wrath really is? Further, how does the title "the prayer of Moses" relate to the nature of Psalm 90 as the corporate prayer of the whole people? Is there significance to a prayer ascribed to Moses being found in a book that is otherwise dominated by David? Further, how do the circumstances of humanity in general in vv. 1-12 relate to the series of requests by the servants of the LORD in vv. 13-17? The transition between them seems quite abrupt. Can these two parts of the prayer be connected together more closely? What impact would these questions have on understanding the request to learn how to count our days in order to gain a wise heart? Answers to these questions and others like them require more than a simple reading of the text, even one that is grounded in the context of committed Christian worship and discipleship.

The Christian Bible, both Old Testament and New Testament, is the church's book. Members of the Christian community can read, interpret, and apply it for themselves, and they are obligated to do so. The Bible has added depths and layers of meaning, however, that do not yield themselves without effortful and expert study using all the resources available to the church in the contemporary world. Nor should the church presume to know all that there is to be known about the Scripture based on a shared communal reading alone. The unfamiliar elements of biblical texts invite further investigation using the accumulated tools of expert study. An initial conversation about Psalm 90 with the church creates many points of contact and affirmation, but it also raises additional questions and stimulates a desire for further clarity and deeper understanding. This desire for greater understanding that arises from the common sense of Scripture calls for another conversation. A conversation with scholars of the Bible is needed. It is to this conversation about the critical sense of the text that we now turn.

Chapter 4

The Critical Sense of the Text: A Conversation with Biblical Scholars

Interpretation of the Bible begins in the church in conversation with the Christian community's understanding of the basic story about God, humanity, and the world. The common sense of Psalm 90 hears this psalm as a communal prayer that laments the brevity of human life, confesses the reality of divine judgment, and pleads for God's compassion and mercy. The Genesis story of God's punishment of human sinfulness informs this interpretation, as does the Exodus story's portrayal of Moses as a bold intercessor on behalf of the covenant people. Within the context of the Christian canon, the prayer for God's grace and mercy is understood through the life and work of Jesus. In Christian faith, the life, death, and resurrection of Jesus are the definitive events that demonstrate God's drawing near to humanity with compassion and grace. The concluding prayer, "let the favor of the Lord our God be upon us, and prosper for us the work of our hands," seeks God's continued blessing and support for the community's continuing service to God.

Though the Christian community has many resources for interpreting Psalm 90 within the context of its worship, history, and practice of ministry, the common sense of the text does not express the fullness of its meaning. Chapter 3 noted a number of lingering questions about details in Psalm 90. Answers to these questions reveal themselves only through careful study of the text in its original language and with the benefit of an accumulated tradition of historical and linguistic investigation. No one tradition contains absolute knowledge. Every perspective has its blind spots that require the benefits of alternative points of view. The critical study of the text that has taken place and continues to take place in educational institutions and scholarly societies provides abundant resources to supplement Christian communities in their interpretation of Scripture.

In his pastoral hermeneutics of Scripture, Gabriel Fackre located the value of critical study of Scripture within the theological doctrine of general revelation. The Christian doctrine of creation recognizes that scholars who work outside of the church or who are not constrained by commitments to Christian teaching and devotion nevertheless possess a common grace given to all who are made in the image of God.[58] This common grace provides the capacity to understand and respond to God, including the knowledge that comes from study of God's human creatures and their languages, cultures, histories, and ideas. The doctrine of revelation also takes into account the Bible's portrayal of human fallenness and its distorting effects on all knowledge, including the church's own understanding of its Scriptures. Christian faith does not exempt believers from the lingering effects that sin has on their thoughts and actions. A desire for worldly status, the ingrained habits of personal autonomy, and the corrupting effects of political and economic power can produce, and often have produced, self-serving interpretations of Scripture in the church. Critical study can provide a necessary correction to the church's self-interested interpretations and intellectual blind spots. The presence of the wisdom tradition in the Bible, an international movement based on human observation and reason, attests to the church's need for the broad traditions of human wisdom that are the result of sharing a common creation.

The long history of the church and the extended transmission of Scripture across centuries, continents, and cultures require a special labor of study and a special set of critical skills to preserve, translate, and interpret ancient texts for new contexts in ways that reflect the fullness of their historical and culturally conditioned nature. The critical study of Scripture is appropriate to the human dimension of its composition and transmission within and across languages and cultures.

In spite of the necessity and appropriateness of critical study, the use of critical tools and methods has been described in both positive and negative ways in Christian communities. Positively, critical study helps to provide important historical, linguistic, and cultural background for issues that are embedded within the texts themselves. For example, when Ps 90:4 describes a thousand years in God's eyes as "a watch in the night," historical evidence for ancient societies' practice of dividing the night into multiple units of time for defensive purposes helps modern readers understand this comparison. Critical study of Scripture requires expert skill and knowledge in evaluating the content of ancient copies of the text, in translating ancient Hebrew, Aramaic, and Greek, and in supplementing allusions to historical events, people, places, and customs with information from ancient sources.

In addition to this positive use of scholarship, critical study has a second, negative connotation. The negative perception of criticism includes conclusions about the historical origins of biblical texts and about the historical accuracy of biblical narratives. These conclusions often seek to correct or contradict the representation of origins or events in the text itself. In this approach, ancient representations of authorship and history are evaluated negatively according to modern concepts of authorship and modern methods of historiography. The goal of this kind of criticism is not to understand the content of the biblical text as written but rather to use the text as a source of information for historical reconstruction. Scholarly reconstruction of ancient history is an important field of study and is beneficial for some aspects of biblical studies. Problems arise, however, when biblical study is reduced to the task of using the Bible for the goal of reconstructing ancient history. The use of critical tools for the goal of illuminating the text is an important and necessary work for responsible biblical study. The use of critical tools and methods to reconstruct a history behind the text or to reconstruct the historical development of the text may in some cases be useful, but the value of such study for the church diminishes to the degree that the goal of study becomes something other than understanding the text.

As discussed in chapter 2, the critical study of the Bible has in recent decades been subjected to the same critical consciousness and hermeneutics of suspicion that scholars had earlier applied to the Bible itself. Critical scholarship is neither completely objective nor disinterested. Its results need to be subjected to careful scrutiny from multiple perspectives, including the perspective of the church's faith claims. Fackre stated his confidence, however, that "[c]riticism of Scripture that rises out of the Christian community, working within its narrative, taking up responsibility within its life, is of special value in strengthening the Body of Christ's vitality."[59]

A critical study of Psalm 90 has two major benefits. First, critical study can address the questions raised by the common sense of the text and expand the church's understanding of Psalm 90 beyond what is available to Christian readers through their own resources alone. Second, critical study of Psalm 90 can serve as an example of the methodologies and skills of exegesis that can be applied to all biblical texts.

There are several resources that guide students of the Bible through the methods of critical biblical exegesis. One of the most widely used resources is John H. Hayes and Carl R. Holladay's book *Biblical Exegesis*.[60] Hayes and Holladay bring together the various critical methodologies that scholars apply to biblical texts and combine them into a comprehensive scheme of interpretation. An alternative approach that describes critical exegesis as more of a process of analysis and synthesis is Michael Gorman's *Elements of Biblical Exegesis*. Gorman's categories provide a logical and holistic approach to exegesis that serves as a clear model for critical analysis of biblical texts.

A sound critical analysis involves addressing multiple questions. It is essential to evaluate the various forms of the text that have been preserved in the oldest and best manuscripts and translations. Contextual analysis seeks to identify the historical circumstances that influenced the text's composition and content. Contextual analysis also examines the literary setting in which the text is found and the cultural setting that helped to produce the text. Formal analysis identifies the type of literature or speech represented by the text and also its structure and the shape of its argument. Detailed analysis investigates the specific language, imagery, and ideas of the text. Once the major elements of the text are identified, critical analysis seeks to establish a synthesis of the meaning of the text from the clues that have been gathered in the research process. Critical analysis of Psalm 90 provides an example of the elements of exegesis in action.

CHOOSING THE BEST HEBREW TEXT OF PSALM 90

The critical study of Scripture is based on technical knowledge and advanced tools that require more preparation and study than the general membership of the church is able to pursue. The clearest example of this is the study of the original languages of the Bible and its textual transmission across the long span of Christian history. The text of Psalm 90 is therefore an important place to begin critical study.

Like much of the Hebrew Bible, the Hebrew manuscripts of Psalm 90 are uniform in the content of the Hebrew text that they preserve. Some different readings occur in ancient translations such as the Greek, Syriac, and Aramaic versions. Most of these examples, however, appear to be changes made in order to provide better readings of a Hebrew text that was difficult to understand or contained uncertain wording in several places. For example, v. 2 describes the creation of the earth using the metaphor of birth: "Before the mountains were born, or before you gave birth to the earth and the world, from everlasting to everlasting, you are God." The second verb, *techolel* in Hebrew, is an active verb whose subject could be either God or "the earth and the world." The phrase could possibly be translated "or before the earth and the world gave birth." The problems with this translation are that, first, the verb is singular and the compound subject "the earth and the world" would usually require a plural verb, and, second, there is no object to identify what the earth gave birth to. The most obvious translation is to take the pronoun "you," referring to God, as the subject of the verb. The problem with this translation, however, is that the use of the imagery of a mother in labor to describe God's act of creation is unusual. The Greek translation, the Latin translation of Jerome, and the Aramaic Targum translate the verb as a passive verb with the earth and the world as the subject. ("Before the earth and the world were brought forth . . . .") The imagery of God giving birth to the world, however, is not unprecedented in the Old Testament. For example, Deuteronomy 32:18, another poetic text attributed to Moses, uses the same Hebrew verb to describe God giving birth to the people of Israel. Similarly, Job 38:8 describes God's creation of the sea as the result of it "burst[ing] out from the womb." The Greek, Aramaic, and Latin translations, therefore, seem most likely to be changes at the translation stage to avoid the description of God as giving birth to creation rather than being evidence of a different Hebrew text. The Hebrew text of v. 2, translated "you gave birth to the earth and the world," represents the best text of this verse.

Another example of a difficult text is in the first two words in v. 5, translated literally as "you sweep them away, sleep." Most translations treat the second word as a result of God's action (NIV, "you sweep them away in the sleep of death") or as an image of impermanence (KJV, "they are as a sleep"; NRSV, "they are like a dream"). Both the Greek and Syriac translations indicate the translators' difficulty understanding the phrase, but neither points to a text that was different from the Hebrew text. Due to the difficulties of the Hebrew, several scholars recommend correcting the Hebrew text by changing a single letter in the first word and changing the vowels of the second word in order to produce a text that means "you sow them yearly."[61] Over the last three decades, however, scholars have become increasingly reluctant to accept changes to the Hebrew text that have no supporting evidence in ancient manuscripts. Verse 5 is difficult, but the imagery of being swept away into the sleep of death, or of sleep as a fleeting state that vanishes suddenly upon awakening, supports the general description of human life as brief and fragile. The Hebrew text of v. 5 is the best text.

One final example of a possible textual variant is in v. 11. The Hebrew text reads, "Who knows the power of your anger, and like the fear of you is your wrath." As discussed above, the second half of the verse is difficult to understand. What does it mean that God's wrath is like the fear of God? Numerous scholars have concluded that the original text has been lost in the process of transmission and that later scribes tried to make the best sense they could out of the corrupted text that was handed down. The Greek translation of v. 11 reads as if the underlying Hebrew text had the preposition "from" instead of the preposition "like." This would involve the interchange of two Hebrew letters, *mem* and *kaf,* that were similar in some ancient Hebrew scripts. The change of letters has led some scholars to propose a text that divides the Hebrew letters into different words that repeat the question of the first half of the verse. The result of this differently divided text is "And who perceives the stroke of your wrath?" Although this change has some support in the Greek translation, no ancient version preserves the division of words represented by this proposal.

The different text represented by the Greek translation, however, does provide evidence of a possible solution to the difficulty of this verse. The preposition "from" reflected in the Greek translation is often used in Hebrew to form a comparative expression. It is possible to translate this text as "Who knows the power of your anger? Or whether your wrath is greater than the fear of you?" This translation raises the possibility that the power of God's wrath may be too great for the proper reverence for God ("the fear of you") to overcome. If so, then the community offering this prayer expressed anxiety that all may already be lost because the power of God's wrath is beyond their ability to seek correction through repentance. As I will discuss below, this translation fits well with the immediate context of vv. 7-12. Even if one does not change the text to fit the Greek translation, the text as it stands still contains a comparison between the wrath of God and the fear of God. The use of the preposition "like" indicates correspondence or even equivalence between the fear of God and the wrath of God. The question, "Who knows the power of your anger, and whether your wrath is equal to the fear of you?" would mean that the wrath of God is equal to the proper reverence for God and therefore cancels out any benefit that the fear of God may provide. The result of such an interpretation would be a recapitulation of v. 9: "All of our days pass away under your wrath; our years come to an end like a sigh." The text behind the Greek translation of v. 11 is possibly the preferred text. Even if it is not the better text, however, it helps to clarify the meaning of the Hebrew text as essentially a comparison and a tension between the redemptive power of the fear of God and the punitive power of God's wrath.

CONTEXTUAL ANALYSIS

One of the major contributions of critical study of the Bible has been an emphasis on the role of context in clarifying the meaning of biblical texts. Context helps the reader understand common knowledge shared by the author and intended audience of a biblical text. The author and audience often shared information that was so obvious to each party that many elements of their common background were left unspoken. Readers who come to the text from a different time and a different cultural background do not have the benefit of these shared assumptions. Contextual analysis seeks to reconstruct the shared background of author and audience so that later readers can read the text with a similar level of understanding.

Historical Context

It is usually beneficial to know the chronological time frame in which texts were written in order to understand references to specific events or circumstances. The question of historical context is difficult for the Psalms, however, for several reasons. The Psalms are mainly prayers used by many people across many different time settings. As a result, references to specific people or events are rare. Prayers meant to be used by groups tend to be fairly general in content in order to be appropriated by a large number of people across a broad sweep of time. Even psalms that refer to specific periods or events could be reflecting on those events from a time far removed from the events described. For example, although Psalm 90 mentions Moses, the figure of Moses was revered in ancient Israel for centuries. The psalm could speak of Moses from one of any number of periods in the history of Israel after Moses. For these reasons, conclusions about the historical context of Psalm 90 are likely to be quite broad.

Although v. 1 identifies Psalm 90 as a "prayer of Moses," few critical scholars see this as an indication of authorship. Strict literary authorship was not a category that was important in ancient Near Eastern culture. Texts were often associated with revered figures of the past whose authority was greater than any known figure in the present. Among his many acts of leadership, Moses is described as a worship leader and composer of songs and prayers in texts such as Exodus 15, Deuteronomy 32, and Deuteronomy 33. The nineteenth-century scholar Franz Delitzsch noted numerous verbal parallels between Psalm 90 and Deuteronomy 32 and 33, including some uses of language unique to those texts.[62] Such use, however, could be evidence of a later prayer in the style of Deuteronomy 32–33, which is the conclusion of most modern scholars.

The ascription of Psalm 90 to Moses has at least two primary implications for the psalm. The first is that it indicates a high level of esteem for the psalm on the part of those who transmitted it. It is associated with one of the most revered figures in Israelite history. Second, the ascription to Moses invites the praying community to read the psalm imaginatively against the background of the story of Moses and his role in Israel's sacred history. The story of Moses provides a framework for imagining the kind of situation that the prayer in Psalm 90 addresses.

Most modern commentators identify the origin of Psalm 90 at some time after the Babylonian exile. The complaints in v. 9 that "all our days pass away under your wrath" and "all our years come to an end like a sigh," and the request in v. 15 to "make us glad as many days as you have afflicted us, and as many years as we have seen evil," suggest a long period of time under conditions that the community interprets as evidence of divine wrath. A long life span of seventy or even eighty years is described in v. 10 as "only toil and trouble." Verses 5-6 compare the brevity of human life to desert grass that flourishes with the morning dew and withers in the afternoon sun. A similar comparison is used in Isaiah 40:6-8, a text set in the time of the Babylonian exile. Verses 13 and 16 include petitions on behalf of "the servants of the LORD." A group referring to themselves as the servants of the LORD appears in postexilic texts like Malachi 3:18; 4:4 and Isaiah 56:6; 65:8-9, 13-15.[63] The many years spent in exile and subjugation to foreign powers following the fall of Jerusalem fit with the general situation described in the psalm, that of a long period of suffering without a clear sign of relief on the horizon.

Literary Context

The idea that the general circumstances of the long postexilic period under foreign rule is the most reasonable setting for Psalm 90 is supported by the literary context of the psalm. Psalm 90 begins Book IV of the Psalms, a collection that includes Psalms 90–106. It follows Psalm 89 at the conclusion of Book III, a psalm that bitterly laments the fall of the Davidic monarchy. Several key words in Psalm 90 connect thematically to language at the end of Psalm 89, especially vv. 46-49. Like Psalm 90:13, Psalm 89:46 asks, "How long, O LORD?" It also strikes another theme of Psalm 90, the wrath of God. "How long will your wrath burn like fire?" Verses 47-48 underscore the urgency of the complaint by pointing to the brevity of the petitioner's life: "Remember my brief life span. Remember how insubstantial you have created all human beings! Who can live and not see death, or deliver his life from Sheol?" Finally, v. 49 asks what has happened to the steadfast love of the LORD, the same divine quality that Psalm 90:14 asks God to restore.

Since the publication of Gerald H. Wilson's book *The Editing of the Hebrew Psalter*, many scholars have accepted the thesis that Book IV of Psalms is an edited compilation that sought to respond to the needs of the postexilic community after the catastrophic loss of the Davidic monarchy and the Jerusalem temple.[64] In the context of the macrostructure of the book of Psalms, Psalm 90 begins Book IV by providing a response to the problem of the failure of the Davidic covenant, which is the primary problem addressed in Psalm 89 at the end of Book III. The figure of Moses is prominent in Book IV. Seven of the eight total references to Moses in the Psalms occur in Psalms 90–106. Psalm 90 is especially prominent as the initial psalm of Book IV and as the only psalm attributed to Moses. Along with Psalm 90, three references to Moses in Psalm 106 (vv. 16, 23, 32) bracket Book IV as a collection featuring the figure of Moses. The time of Moses was a time when God, not David or a Davidic king, reigned directly over Israel and when the presence of God provided direct refuge for the covenant people before the institutions of temple or monarchy were established.[65] Book IV expresses the concerns of a disenfranchised community who nevertheless believes that God is still on their side.[66] This postexilic Jewish community sought divine help to cope with a lengthy period of subjugation under foreign powers by looking for inspiration in the leadership and provision God gave to Israel in the time of Moses.

FORMAL ANALYSIS

Ancient Israelite worshipers used various kinds of prayers for various occasions and needs. Some prayers made urgent requests of God while others offered thanksgiving for help received or celebrated God's goodness and greatness. Analyzing the category of prayer that a particular psalm falls into, its form, is helpful in knowing what its authors and audience expected the psalm to say and do.

Scholars describe the form of Psalm 90 in two related but distinctive ways. The basic category is the communal prayer for help. The entire psalm is addressed to God as a prayer. It uses the first person plural voice of the entire congregation, from the first line, "O Lord, you have been *our* dwelling place," to the concluding words, "prosper for *us* the works of *our* hands." Either the entire congregation prayed the prayer together, or a worship leader voiced the prayer on behalf of the people as a whole. Examples of communal prayers for help include Psalms 44, 60, 74, 79, and 80. Typically, the communal prayer for help laments a crisis that has overtaken the community and implores God to intervene decisively in the people's favor.

Psalm 90 has the overall form of a communal prayer for help. It begins with a statement of trust in God. It ends with a series of petitions for God's intervention, mercy, and favor. Other typical elements of a communal prayer for help are either absent or understated, however. While other communal prayers for help refer to wars, famines, or other imminent disasters, there is no explicit description in Psalm 90 of the crisis that threatens the community.[67] The primary complaint is that God's persistent wrath threatens to overwhelm the reasonable life span of each member of the community.

The general nature of the complaint in Psalm 90 suggests to some that the form of the psalm is primarily that of a meditation on the general condition of human life as brief and troubled, presented in the form of a communal prayer for help. Gerhard von Rad argued that the content of Psalm 90 was closest to the book of Ecclesiastes' description of the futility of human life.[68] Tate argued that Psalm 90 was a literary composition that used the form of a communal prayer for help as an artistic device to offer a meditation on how devout worshipers could learn to cope with "hard times long endured."[69] Gerstenberger labeled the form of Psalm 90 a communal meditation. He argued that it was the work of professional liturgists who used prayer forms and worship settings to impart their reflections on philosophical and existential issues as a way of instructing and encouraging the Jewish communities who suffered under long and indefinite periods of foreign rule.[70]

The view of Psalm 90 as a meditation in the form of a prayer focuses on the generalized nature of the complaints in vv. 3-10 regarding the brevity and harshness of human life, and on the request in v. 12 that concludes the first major section of the psalm: "Teach us to count our days that we may gain a wise heart." In this interpretation, a proper evaluation of the brevity of life based on divinely given wisdom is the psalm's proposal for coping with life's anxieties.

Other scholars, however, argue that the external form of the communal prayer for help is not simply an artistic device, but rather reflects the true nature and purpose of the psalm. Richard Clifford has argued that the psalm as a whole fits with the expectations and the elements of a communal lament.[71] The key to this conclusion is the question of what the psalmist is asking for when he asks in v. 12 for God to "teach us to count our days." The traditional answer, the answer as understood by most religious readers, is that the prayer asks for an understanding of the brevity of life and the wisdom to live appropriately. Verses 3-10, however, make clear that the psalmist already knows that human life is short and subject to divine wrath. Clifford interpreted vv. 11-12 in light of evidence in biblical and ancient Near Eastern texts of a widespread expectation that divine judgment often had defined time limits and that these time limits were often communicated through prophetic oracles.[72] Clifford proposed that the question in v. 11, "Who considers the power of your anger?" was a question about the duration of God's wrath rather than its force. He then described v. 12 as a request for knowledge of the time limit of wrath in order to live out the remaining days appropriately, that is to say, with "a wise heart." According to Clifford, v. 12 is a request for God to reveal, presumably through a prophetic oracle, the literal number of days that God's wrath would persist.

Clifford's explanation of vv. 11-12 allows the entire psalm to conform to the expectations of a communal prayer for help. Verses 1-2 begin with a statement of confidence in God's past protection and creative power. Verses 3-6, a description of the brevity of life, provide motivation for God to answer the prayer. Though God has an eternal frame of reference, the brevity of life calls for an answer to the cry for help before the praying community's time expires. Verses 7-10 provide the formal complaint. God's wrath, though justified, threatens to consume all of the days allotted to the congregation if it is not limited. Verses 11-12 ask for knowledge of the appointed duration of suffering, with the hope that wrath is not the final word. Verses 13-17 extend this hope through petitions for God to relent from wrath and turn back toward the community with steadfast love, with the specific request that their time of rejoicing might at least be equal to if not exceed their time of affliction.

The general nature of the community's condition, a long period of dislocation and submission, and the connection between the two distinct topics of the brevity of life and divine wrath give the psalm a reflective and didactic tone. When set within the historical context of the long period of displacement after the exile and within the literary context of Book IV of the Psalms, the form of Psalm 90 as a communal prayer for help comes into greater focus. The image of Moses, the great intercessor of ancient Israel as seen for example in Exodus 32:12-13, adds weight to the form of the text as a communal prayer for help. In Psalm 90, the community is taught to pray during its long sojourn in exile and subjugation in the manner that Moses prayed in the wilderness when he implored God to repent of wrath and turn back toward God's people in mercy.

STRUCTURAL ANALYSIS

Careful attention to the precise language of Psalm 90 yields indications of its rhetorical structure and artful design. The content of the psalm and the elements of the form of communal lament already provide a clear outline.

I. Statement of trust in God's protection and power in past generations (vv. 1-2)
II. The brevity of human life compared with God's unlimited time horizon (vv. 3-6)
III. The problem of God's prolonged wrath (vv. 7-10)
IV. Complaint: Should prolonged wrath render repentance null and void? (vv. 11-12)
V. Petitions for time of renewal proportionate to past afflictions (vv. 13-15)
VI. Petitions for God's saving power and protection for future generations (vv. 16-17)

Thematic connections and repetition of key words within and between the major units of the psalm create an artful and logical progression for the argument the prayer is making. A community that has suffered long under God's wrath seeks relief and a return to the shelter of God's powerful and life-giving presence as it was experienced long ago.

The opening section of the prayer in vv. 1-2 is defined by its prayerful address to God in praise. Names or titles for God, accompanied by the pronoun "you," begin and end the section ("Lord, a dwelling place you have been . . . you are God").[73] This outer frame brackets parallel references to time ("from generation to generation . . . from everlasting to everlasting"), parallel references to major elements of creation ("the mountains . . . the earth and the world"), and parallel verbs for the process of creation ("were born . . . you gave birth").[74]

Verses 3-6 are bracketed by a pair of verbs in the same Hebrew conjugation in which the consonants *shin* and *bet* appear in inverted order (*tasheb . . . veyabesh*). Thus, the unit begins with "You return humankind to dust" and ends with "it [i.e., grass, a metaphor for humans] withers and dries up." The verb *shub* ("return"), which is used twice in v. 3, is echoed in v. 13 in the second half of the psalm. In v. 3, God returns humans to dust and says to them "turn back," while in v. 13 the community asks God to "turn back" from wrath to mercy. The phrase "in the morning" occurs in vv. 5-6 and v. 14. In vv. 5-6 it describes the brevity of human life as being like grass that flourishes "in the morning." In v. 14 it describes the time when God is asked to satisfy the community's needs with steadfast love so that they can rejoice in all their days.[75]

Verses 7-10 are set apart from vv. 3-6 by a return to the use of first person plural pronouns for the praying community and by the use of the second person singular pronoun for God: "We are consumed . . . by your wrath . . . you have set our iniquities before you." This section is connected to vv. 13-15 by the words "all our days" (v. 9, 14) and by the word pair "days and years" (v. 9, 15).[76]

Verses 11-12 form the center point of the psalm, as indicated by the verbal links between vv. 3-10 and vv. 13-15 before and after these verses. Within this unit, the two poetic verses are connected by the use of the verb "to know" ("Who knows . . . make us know . . ."). The phrase "our days" in v. 12 connects this verse to the sections before (v. 9) and after (v. 14). At the juncture of vv. 11 and 12, the prayer shifts from complaint to petition. This transition forms the hinge or turning point of the psalm.[77]

Verses 13-15 continue the form of petitions begun in v. 12. The distinctiveness of this unit is marked in v. 13, however, by new expressions for the major figures in the psalm. Here God is identified for the only time in the psalm by the divine name Yahweh, which is indicated in our English translations by the word "LORD" in small uppercase letters. The community is identified for the first time as "your servants." The meaning of the imperative verb "turn" that begins v. 13 is fleshed out in the content of vv. 14-15, which describe a change in circumstances from trouble and evil (v. 15) to steadfast love and rejoicing (v. 14). The use of the verb "turn" to invoke the mercy of God also contrasts with the use of this verb in v. 3 as a decree of God that sets God and humanity at a distance.

Petitions continue in vv. 16 and 17. These verses stand apart from vv. 13-15, however, by beginning their requests with the use of third person subjunctive verbs ("let your work be manifest . . . and let the favor of the Lord our God be upon us").[78] The request that the glory of the Lord be shown to the children of God's servants in the future creates a ring structure for the psalm as a whole by balancing the description in v. 1 of God as a dwelling place "in all generations" past. Dennis Tucker has identified another verbal link between v. 17 and v. 1 in the key word "favor" (Hebrew *no'am*).[79] This word is a reversal of the consonants of the word "dwelling place" (Hebrew *ma'on*) in v. 1. The effect of this device is to illustrate the desired effect of the prayer. As the Lord had been a dwelling place in previous generations, the petition asks that the current situation of wrath be reversed so that the community may come to experience again the favor of the Lord.[80] The third person subject of the verb at the beginning of v. 17 ("let the favor of the Lord our God be upon us") gives it a form similar to a benediction, drawing the prayer to a conclusion on a hopeful note of trust.

The careful construction and artistry of Psalm 90 demonstrate why some critical scholars have considered it to be a literary composition from a circle of learned scribes similar to the Jewish sage Jesus Ben Sira, the author of the deuterocanonical book of Ecclesiasticus, who was active at the end of the third and beginning of the second centuries BCE.[81] The artistry within the psalm served the rhetorical purposes of expressing the needs and hopes of a worshiping community through a communal prayer that sought to effect a change in God and also in the praying community. Tucker has argued that the rhetoric of Psalm 90 sets forth an itinerary from exile to return, from the memory of protection in past generations to a cry for God to return in mercy and favor for the benefit of the present community and for their future descendants.[82]

DETAILED ANALYSIS

The background, form, structure, and movement of Psalm 90 reveal that it is a communal prayer for help on behalf of a community enduring a long period of suffering with no apparent relief on the horizon. The prayer laments that the duration of God's wrath has no clear endpoint in sight. This situation threatens to sentence the community to a life of trouble and futility for the entirety of their brief life span. In response, the community petitions God to turn back to them with compassion so that they and their descendants may once again experience God's favor. Having explored the setting and the broad outline of the prayer, it is helpful now for us to clarify the specific details that support and fill out this picture.

The prayer of Moses, the man of God.[83] As noted above, Moses, the preeminent leader in Israel's history, is an important figure in Book IV of the Psalms that includes Psalms 90–106. As a collection that responds to the fall of the Davidic monarchy and the loss of temple, land, and kingdom, Book IV looks to the time of Moses when God led the people directly as their king and provided refuge and protection for them through the wilderness. Moses also plays a prominent role in Psalm 90 as the model for the petitions in v. 13. In Exodus 32, Moses boldly interceded for the people threatened with destruction for their worship of a golden calf, petitioning God to "turn from the fury of your anger and repent concerning disaster toward your people." Exodus 32:12 and Psalm 90:13 are the only two texts in the Hebrew Bible that address the words "turn" and "repent" to God in a prayer.[84] Both prayers in Exodus 32 and Psalm 90 ask God for mercy so that God's punishment does not exceed the measure that the people are able to bear. In Psalm 90, the community is taught to pray in the manner of Moses, whose bold intercession turned back God's wrath.

O Lord, a dwelling place you have been for us in generation after generation. The prayer begins with an acknowledgment of the relationship between the community and God. The people address God with the title "Lord" and pray as God's subjects and servants.[85] The relationship between people and God is also described by the metaphor of dwelling place or refuge. In the postexilic background of this prayer, the people have lost the security of king, kingdom, land, and temple. The invocation of the age of Moses in the title remembers a time when God was shelter, refuge, and protector of the people without the mediating institutions of king or temple.

The acknowledgment that God has been a dwelling place for the people in all generations contains both an affirmation and a hint of complaint. The affirmation is that God's presence and protection have been the hope of the people across the span of a long history. The complaint is that this protection is described as fixed in the past. The use of the verb *hayah* ("to be") in the perfect conjugation suggests that this protective relationship either hangs in suspense or has already ceased at a time in the past.[86] The sense of v. 1 is that God *was* a refuge in generations *past*. The question that the prayer raises is whether the same can be said for the present or future generations.

Before the mountains were born, or you gave birth to the earth and the world, from everlasting to everlasting, you are God. The affirmation of God's power and provision extends far beyond the history of Israel to include the whole of creation. The sovereign lord of the community is also the eternal creator of all. As noted above, the description of creation is cast in imagery that is unusual though not unprecedented in Hebrew Scripture. God is the one who "gave birth" to the earth and the world. The two verbs used here, *yalad* and *hil*, are also used in Deuteronomy 32:18, another song of Moses, to describe the creation of Israel. Moses used similar language in Numbers 11:12 to complain about the unfair burden of leading the people through the wilderness. "Did I *conceive* all this people? Did I *give birth* to them, that you should say to me, 'Carry them in your bosom, as a nurse carries a sucking child' . . . ?" (emphasis added). The assumption of this complaint is that it is God, not Moses, who "gave birth" to the people, metaphorically speaking. The imagery of God giving birth to creation also has the effect of describing the intimate nature of the relationship between God and God's people. The emphasis on the closeness between God and people is similar in effect to the language of Isaiah 49:14-15: "But Zion said, 'The LORD has forsaken me, my Lord has forgotten me.' Can a woman forget her nursing child, or show no compassion for the child of her womb? Even these may forget, yet I will not forget you." The metaphor of giving birth to describe the relationship between creator and creation, used in Isaiah 49 to remind the exiles of God's compassion, is used in Psalm 90 in a communal lament to remind God of the same relationship.

You return little humans to dust and you say, "Turn back, O mortals." For a thousand years in your eyes are like a single yesterday that fades away, and like a watch in the night. The theme of God's eternal existence introduced in vv. 1-2 is extended in v. 3 by contrasting it with the limited nature of human life. The word translated "dust" evokes God's statement to Adam and Eve in Genesis 3: "You are dust, and to dust you shall return" (v. 19). Though the word used in Psalm 90 is a different one, the effect is the same as in Genesis 3. Humans, creatures of earth, are finite beings, living within the temporal and physical limits set by the eternal God. God and humans, therefore, operate on different time horizons. Human time is fleeting. It passes like yesterday that is gone and like a watch of the night that passes while most people are asleep. God, meanwhile, has all the time in the world. The portrayal of the relationship between Lord and people introduced in vv. 1-2 takes on added dimensions. The praying community seeks God as the descendants of generations who have lived under God's protection, as the precious children of God's own womb, as it were, and as frail human beings whose lives are like meteors that flash across the night sky and then disappear. What is not urgent for God as creator of both the world and of time is nevertheless extremely urgent for the community who experiences life as finite creatures occupying a fleeting moment in the sweep of history.

You sweep them away. They become like sleep in the morning, like the grass that fades away. In the morning, it flourishes but passes away. At evening it withers and dries up. Verses 5 and 6 add new imagery to illustrate the theme of urgent need introduced in v. 3. These lines present a montage of images of things that quickly pass away. The verb *zmm* connotes a flood that sweeps away what lies in its path. The sleep that lasts for hours dissolves into nothing upon awakening in the morning. Like v. 4, the image of grass that flourishes with the morning dew but withers in the afternoon sun uses the span of a single day to describe the brevity of human life in comparison to God. The cumulative effect of vv. 3-6 is to support the community's need for divine help by contrasting their limited time horizon as mere mortals to the limitless time frame in which God may choose to act.

Having described the community's relationship to God and the urgency of their need, the unit containing vv. 7-10 describes their over-riding problem: "All our days pass away in your wrath" (v. 9). While vv. 3-6 spoke in general terms about human beings, using third person pronouns "they" and "them," vv. 7-10 return to the use of the first person plural pronouns "we," and "our." The community prays as a people living under the wrath of God: "Indeed, we are consumed by your anger, and over-whelmed by your wrath. You have set our iniquities before you, our hidden things before the light of your face." The prayer does not dispute the justice of God's judgment. The terms "wrath" and "anger" describe the effects of divine judgment by using human emotions to describe a God who cannot be described except by stretching ordinary language. The praying commu-nity does not contest the exposure of their wrongfulness in the light of God's presence. They do, however, complain about the duration of judg-ment that consumes their entire lifetime: "All our days pass away in your wrath; we bring our years to an end like a sigh. The number of years may be seventy years or if by strength eighty years, yet their result is toil and trouble. It is soon gone, and we fly away" (vv. 9-10). Interpreting vv. 7-10 as the complaint of a communal prayer for help, the seventy and eighty years are not intended to describe the average human life span but the maximum time span that members of the community might hope to endure. Even such long lives, however, are embittered by the experience of divine judgment that seems unrelenting.

A text from the book of Zechariah in reference to the desolation of Jerusalem provides background for the view that vv. 7-10 are a complaint about an indefinite period of judgment. In Zechariah 1:7-17, the prophet reports a vision received in the year 520 BCE, roughly seventy years after the destruction of Jerusalem. In the vision, the angel of the LORD offers a prayer of lament on behalf of Jerusalem: "O LORD of hosts, how long will you withhold mercy from Jerusalem and the cities of Judah, with which you have been angry these seventy years?" (Zech 1:12) The angel's lament, reflecting the views of the people of Jerusalem, is that the period of God's anger toward Jerusalem had lasted for the appointed time of seventy years and should therefore come to an end. Psalm 90 is a similar prayer, voiced on behalf of the worshiping community, lamenting that their time under divine wrath should not last indefinitely but give way to a new period of restoration.

The complaint about the indefinite and excessive duration of God's judgment reaches its climax in vv. 11-12, although the exact meaning of this unit may have been obscured during the transmission of the text. The language of the first line of v. 11 seems clear enough: "Who knows the power of your anger?" Clifford argues that in the context of the prayer, the word for "power" should be understood as the duration of God's anger.[87] The second line literally reads, "like the fear of you your wrath." "The fear of you" refers to "the fear of God," expressed with the personal pronoun "you" because it is addressed to God in prayer. The fear of God is an idiom that describes not an emotion but rather a disposition of respect and obedience toward God. In some contexts, it is a technical term for piety. Similar uses of the phrase "fear of you" are found in Deuteronomy 2:25; Isaiah 63:17; Psalms 5:8; 119:38; and Job 4:6; 22:4. The line compares the wrath that God expresses toward people to the reverence and obedience that people express toward God. What is unclear in v. 11 is how these two are comparable.

Clifford concluded that the meaning of the second half of v. 11 has been corrupted in the process of textual transmission and cannot be satisfactorily recovered.[88] A possible clue, however, may be found in the text preserved in the Septuagint. Instead of the comparative preposition "like," the Septuagint reads "from the fear of you." The difference between the prepositions "like" and "from" is the difference between the Hebrew letters *kaf* and *mem*, letters that were quite similar in ancient scripts and that caused textual corruptions in multiple passages.[89] The reading of the Greek text, "your wrath is from the fear of you," however, makes little sense. But in Hebrew, the preposition *mem*, "from," is also used to form a comparative expression. A common form of this expression combines the preposition *mem* with an adjective and a noun in a clause that means "more [adjective] than [noun]." Judges 14:18 provides a good example. "What is sweeter than [Heb., "sweet from"] honey? What is stronger than [Heb., "strong from"] a lion?" Waltke and O'Connor point out that in some poetic contexts, the adjective that forms the basis of the comparison is left out and the sense of the comparison must be derived from the context.[90] An example similar in structure to Psalm 90:11 is found in Job 11:17. The literal Hebrew wording reads, "And from noonday a life will rise, darkness will become like the morning." The comparative sense of the preposition "from" in this context means "and *brighter than* noonday a life will rise."

Reading Psalm 90:11 with the text preserved in the Septuagint as "from the fear of you" and translating this text as a comparative expression yields the translation, "your wrath is greater than the fear of you." The translation becomes clearer if the question "Who knows?" in the first half of v. 11 is extended to include the second half: "Who knows the power of your anger, or if your wrath is more powerful than the fear of you?" Read in this way, the verse raises the possibility that the wrath of God is so great that the people's proper fear of God, their reverent obedience, has no positive effect. Divine wrath threatens to render an appropriate human response futile. This reading fits into the context of the preceding complaint that God's wrath threatens to consume the community's entire span of life.

Verse 11 continues the complaint of vv. 7-10 and focuses it into a question of theodicy. Should the wrath of God be so powerful that the people's fear of God comes to no good effect, rendered void by unrelenting judgment? This question is the central point of tension in the prayer. Verse 12 expresses the people's resistance to the idea raised in v. 11 that wrath may be God's final word. In this verse, the prayer turns from complaint to petition: "Let us know how to count our days rightly that we may gain a wise heart." Clifford points out that the Hebrew word *ken* can be translated not only as "so" but also as the adverb "rightly." Verse 11 suggests that God's wrath might be so powerful that the people's fear of God has no effect. Verse 12 asks for information that would correct this conclusion so that the community could live out their days wisely. It is a request that the apparent conflict between the community's expectation of God and their current situation be resolved in a way that honors God's character and rewards the people's faith.

The verb in v. 12 translated "gain" literally means "to bring in." This verb can have two connotations. One is agriculture, as in bringing in a harvest. The other connotation is "to bring as an offering; to offer." Learning how long God's wrath would endure might allow the community to reap the harvest of a wise heart during the time of judgment that remains. Alternately, learning that God's wrath has a specific limit would encourage the community to fear God and therefore offer to God in worship the sacrifice of a wise heart. Since most offerings were the result of agricultural harvest, the two interpretations are similar. Psalm 51:17 describes a broken and contrite heart as an acceptable sacrifice to God. In light of this imagery, therefore, it is best to translate v. 12 as "Teach us to count our days rightly so that we may bring to you the offering of a wise heart." Knowing the limited duration of God's wrath would allow the community to avoid the conclusion that the fear of God is of no use. Therefore, they could worship God wisely and rightly.

The logical conclusion to the knowledge that the period of wrath had definite limits would be the hope that God would change God's disposition from wrath to mercy. This is exactly what is requested in vv. 13-15: "Turn, O LORD, how long? Have compassion upon your servants. Satisfy us in the morning with your steadfast love that we may be glad and rejoice all our days. Let us rejoice as many days as you have afflicted us, and as many years as we have seen trouble." The key words "turn," "have compassion," "steadfast love," and "all our days" voice a request for a reversal of the situation in which "all our days pass away under your wrath" (v. 9). Although they have endured "years of affliction" (v. 15), the people still identify themselves as God's servants and seek a demonstration of the steadfast, covenantal love that they have experienced.

Verses 16-17 allude to themes from the beginning of the prayer, but from a perspective of hope instead of doubt. The people ask that the saving work and splendor of God be revealed to the present generation and to future generations. This petition recapitulates the remembrance of God's protection in past generations stated in v. 1. It also invokes the power of God as sovereign creator, another theme from the introduction of the psalm. Verse 17 asks for the favor of the Lord to be upon the people. As Tucker observed, this word is a literal reversal of the word "dwelling place" from v. 1. The prayer has moved rhetorically from a doubtful present to a hopeful future. The psalm concludes with a repeated petition that God establish the work of their hands. Since the people make their petitions as God's servants, the work of their hands is a way of describing their service for God. The prayer ends with a request that God will affirm and accept the service that the people render to God. The repetition of this request signals the end of the prayer. People who were led to question whether their best acts of fidelity, their "fear of God," might be of no avail are nevertheless emboldened to ask God to affirm and establish their work with lasting significance. Prayer has moved the community from expressions of doubt and despair to petitions of affirmation and hope.

SYNTHESIS

Study of the contextual, formal, and detailed elements of Psalm 90 reveals a psalm with a clear purpose, form, and thesis. The different parts of the prayer work together to move the reader/participant from a sense of forsakenness and despair to one of trust and hope. The psalm is a prayer for help voiced by a community that has suffered a long period of humiliation and displacement. The best context for understanding the prayer is Israel's long experience of displacement and subordination in the postexilic period. The extended period of life under foreign dominion without meaningful change likely contributed to the general nature of the prayer. It is a prayer about time spent under wrath. This lengthy state is made more problematic because God's horizon is unbounded by time, while the praying community sees its brief life ebbing away entirely under judgment without relief.

The form of a communal prayer holds the entire psalm together with a strong sense of unity. The meditation on the brevity of human life in vv. 3-6 serves as motivation for God to act. The problem that the psalm laments is the prospect of lives lived out under wrath with no apparent end in sight. This circumstance belies the affirmations within Israel's tradition of the essential goodness of life in God's blessed creation. The prayer reaches a point of crisis in v. 11. The community questions whether God's wrath cancels out all faithful responses on the part of a chastened people. Verses 12-15 are a protest based on the community's identity as the covenant people of God and based on the character of God as voluntarily bound by the promise of steadfast, covenanted love. The community prays to know the fixed time of their punishment so that they can worship God confidently and wisely, dismissing the doubts that arise from unrelenting judgment. More important, they pray as Moses prayed on Mount Sinai, "Turn back, O LORD . . . and repent concerning your servants." As God promised through the prophet Joel to restore the years that the locust had devoured, so Psalm 90 prays that the people might rejoice for as many days as God has afflicted them. The prayer concludes with a hope that God will favor future generations as God had done in past generations, and that a turn in God's disposition from wrath to mercy will allow the people to put hope in the fruitfulness of their labor as God's servants.

CONCLUSION: THE COMMON AND CRITICAL SENSES OF THE TEXT

Study of the common sense of the text in conversation with the Christian community highlighted its main ideas and identified important questions that required more specialized study. Conversation with biblical scholars about the critical sense has helped to address these questions. One of the questions addressed the title of the psalm as "the prayer of Moses, the man of God," in a book dominated by the figure of David. Attention to the literary context of Book IV of the Psalms and to the historical and literary setting of Book IV as a response to the fall of the Davidic kingdom and the exile revealed the significance of this title. Book IV looks to the figure of Moses as a symbol of a time when God ruled Israel directly without king, temple, or land. It provides Israel with prayers, hymns, and liturgies for worshiping and trusting God in the long sojourn of the postexilic period by comparing this time with the period of Israel's long sojourn from Egypt to the promised land.

The historical and literary contexts of Psalm 90 also help in understanding the mythological language of creation in v. 2, language that is unlike the description of creation found in Genesis 1–2. Psalm 90 participates in a broader poetic vocabulary of creation than the vocabulary used in the narratives of Genesis. This vocabulary serves to connect Psalm 90 with an earlier period, much in the way that the reference to Moses does in the title of the psalm. The mythological language also evokes a deeper sense of intimacy between creator and creation.

A third question had to do with the negative assessment of life in Psalm 90 as full of "toil and trouble," followed by a hasty death. Critical study shows that this view describes the plight of a particular community, the exilic community of Israel enduring a long, drawn-out time of judgment seemingly without end. Despite its general description of human transience, Psalm 90 is the prayer of a specific community rather than a meditation on human life in general from birth to grave. In vv. 3-6, the community prays as mortals whose time is brief and fleeting, therefore demonstrating the urgency of their need. In vv. 12-17, the community prays consciously as the servants of God who hope and request that God's true nature be revealed as being more like their past affirmations than their present experience.

Critical study also helps to clarify the puzzling comparison in v. 11 between the fear of God and the wrath of God. How are these two comparable? For this question, textual criticism, Hebrew grammar, and formal analysis help to clarify the meaning of an obscure text. Following the text preserved in the Greek translation, I have translated v. 11 as "Who knows the power of your anger, or whether your wrath is greater than the fear of you?" Verse 11 asks whether the wrath of God, the focus of the community's complaint in vv. 7-10, might be so strong that it cancels out any benefit of the fear of God, rendering futile the people's appropriate response to God and forestalling any wisdom that the fear of God might engender. In the face of such a grave threat, the psalm turns immediately to a series of petitions that beseech God to demonstrate that things are not as they appear but are rather the final moments of gloom before the reprieve of a saving dawn.

The common sense of Psalm 90 is strongly influenced by its general language and broad themes of creation, time, human frailty, and divine wrath. These give the psalm the sense of being a meditation on universal human transience in contrast to God's eternal nature. The elements to support this interpretation are all present in the text, and the church is not wrong to hear these themes sounded or to use the psalm as commentary on these ideas. Critical study does not contradict the common sense so much as integrate the individual elements of the psalm into a clearer context and a more unified and holistic literary structure. The psalm functions holistically as a prayer of a particular community with a particular need. It reveals that a crisis that unfolds slowly over decades is no less of a crisis for the gradual nature of its unfolding. Years of languishing without a sign of hope erode faith and corrode trust. Psalm 90 draws strength from the spirit of Moses and the deep tradition of Israel in order not to give in to a despairing sense of futile faithfulness. The critical sense of Scripture adds depth, dimension, movement, and unity to the ideas that rest on the surface of the text. Critical scholarship is a gift to the church that allows it to hear the message of Psalm 90 in stereo and high definition. It supports and also corrects and extends the church's reading by inviting the church to identify with worshiping communities living not just under the existential threat of death but also under the shadow of indefinite "wrath" during the finite days of its communal life.

One of the most important contributions of the critical sense of Psalm 90 is the way that it highlights the specific history and literary expressions of the people of Israel. The general themes of creation and the brevity of human life can give the psalm a sense of universalism that diminishes the unique perspective and experience of the people of Israel. Critical study locates the psalm in the particular history and thought world of Israel's postexilic circumstances, reflected through the lens of their long-standing traditions. Christian readings of the Old Testament have often been quick to diminish the particularity of Israel's Scripture as part of a larger and more harmful tendency to downplay the significance of the Jewish people's enduring faith and continuing existence. The critical sense of Psalm 90 corrects this universalizing tendency and allows Israel's unique experience and voice to be heard more clearly.

Critical study also adds a new depth of specificity and texture to the prayer for knowledge to count one's days in order to gain a wise heart. The specific request is to know that the duration of the period of God's wrath is fixed and numbered. That knowledge would avoid the despair of v. 11 that fearing and worshiping might be of no use. To know the number of the days of wrath would allow the community to offer worship to God from a wise heart and not from a heart of suspicion or bitterness.

For all the value of critical study when used judiciously and faithfully, it is not the final word on the meaning of Scripture. The message received through critical study needs to be brought into the context of the church's full confession of faith concerning the wonder and mystery of God revealed through Israel and Jesus against the backdrop of its two-testament canon. To accomplish this, a wider conversation is needed, one with the broad tradition of the church expressed in its canon and creeds and also in conversation with the work of its theologians who have studied and expounded on these over the centuries. Fackre named this conversation the canonical sense of the text, and it is to this conversation that we now turn.

Chapter 5

The Canonical Sense of the Text: A Conversation with Theologians

Reading Psalm 90 in conversation with the church reveals connections to major biblical themes like creation, covenant, time, eternity, justice, and mercy, but it raises questions that cannot be answered by a straightforward reading alone. Reading Psalm 90 in conversation with biblical scholars clarifies these questions and also brings together the various components of the psalm into an integrated whole. Internal and contextual evidence shows the psalm to be a prayer for help for a community that has suffered a long-term crisis of dislocation and marginalization. It fits well with Israel's postexilic history in which the survivors of the fallen kingdom of Judah lived in minority enclaves across the Persian Empire or in the former land of Judah as a colony under Persian rule. The prayer invokes the voice and stature of Moses, the great leader of Israel in premonarchic times, whose struggle to secure the freedom of the people consumed his entire life and whose boldness before God on behalf of the people finds an echo in the words of the psalm. The deep relationship between Israel and God and the tenacious faith ascribed to Moses led the community to plead for God's mercy when the evidence of their experience alone suggested that only wrath might be expected.

Critical study is beneficial for anchoring Psalm 90 in the concrete circumstances of a particular people and for revealing how the psalm expresses their need. Critical study cannot, however, be the last word in the theological interpretation of the text. The contemporary community who reads Psalm 90 is not the same community for whom it was composed as a communal lament. The faith of contemporary Christian communities who read Psalm 90 as part of their worship, proclamation, devotional study, and ministry is related to the faith of the community behind Psalm 90, but it is not the same faith. Christians approach Psalm 90 as people who see the life, death, and resurrection of Jesus as the decisive moment in human history, bringing believers into a living relationship with God and transforming how they understand all that came before it, including the meaning of the Scriptures passed down through the people of Israel.

A CONVERSATION WITH THEOLOGIANS

In order to make the journey from the biblical "then" to the Christian "now," interpretation must move beyond the common and critical senses of the text to what theologian Gabriel Fackre termed "the canonical sense." The canonical sense refers to the influence that the context of the entire Scripture has on the meaning of individual texts. The existence of a canon of Scripture privileges the content of books included within it and gives them greater influence and authority for the believing community. Scriptural communities receive biblical texts within canonical collections whose orientation, affirmations, and theological perspectives provide a guiding context for understanding and interpreting individual texts. Theological presuppositions guided the creation of a canon, and the use of the canon within religious communities reinforces the theology that shaped the canon.[91]

The theological nature of the canonical sense of the text means that this sense requires a conversation with the church's theologians. This includes the nameless theologians who created the Jewish Scriptures that preceded the church and the Christian theologians who created the Christian canon by acknowledging, expanding, and reinterpreting the Jewish Scriptures within the context of the Christian proclamation about Jesus. It also includes the theologians whose work is reflected in Christian creeds and in the interpretation of Scripture as guided by the creeds across the span of Christian history.

By including a canonical approach within his overall program of theological interpretation, Fackre demonstrated his knowledge of and engagement with a movement in biblical studies that emerged in the early 1970s and has strongly influenced academic and theological interpretation of the Bible. Fackre cites the primary importance of Brevard Childs in the development and influence of the canonical approach in biblical studies. As discussed in Chapter 2, Childs's 1974 commentary on Exodus in the Old Testament Library series was a watershed event in the study of the Old

Testament. In addition to the critical issues related to the reigning method-ologies of biblical studies, he devoted significant attention to what he called the Old Testament Context and the New Testament Context of individual textual units. He also addressed the history of interpretation of each passage in premodern exegesis and summarized the current relevance of each text for Christian readers in a concluding section titled "Theological Reflec-tion." Childs's commentary set the agenda for theological study of the Bible for the decades that followed. Most commentaries since Childs's Exodus commentary have addressed in some manner the matters of the broader canonical context of individual biblical texts, the history of interpretation prior to the advent of modern critical studies, and the theological relevance of the text for contemporary readers. New commentary series have also emerged to address issues such as the reception history of the text or the theological interpretation of the text in great detail.

Childs's commentary and Fackre's discussion of the canonical sense of the text in his pastoral systematics provide an outline of what the canon-ical sense should include. First, connections between the individual text and the broader context of the two testaments of the Christian canon are brought to the foreground at the canonical level of interpretation. The Old Testament and the New Testament receive separate treatment owing to the literary, historical, and theological integrity of each collection.[92] Once the literary context of each canonical testament is addressed, then the text can serve as a point of dialogue between them. The canonical sense also includes a study of the relationship between the text under study and the grand narrative that unifies the two testaments into a single, biblical story of the triune God as embraced in the Christian faith. The church's ecumen-ical creeds provide an outline and a guideline for identifying and following this overarching narrative. In addition to the canonical context and the narrative outline of the faith expressed in the creeds, the interpretation of the text preserved within the history of Christian biblical interpretation provides an additional resource for clarifying the canonical sense of the text.

The following discussion of the canonical sense of Psalm 90 will describe the way that the larger contexts of the Old Testament and the New Testament give added meaning to the content of the psalm. I will also look at the way the psalm has been interpreted theologically by selected teachers of the patristic and Reformation eras. I will then look at the psalm through the lens of the Apostle's Creed. In approaching these contexts for Psalm 90, I want to emphasize the nature of this investigation as a conversation with the church's theologians. I am not a theologian by training. My conviction and the argument of this book, however, is that multiple conversations about Scripture with the church, biblical scholars, theologians, and the world make our understanding and embodiment of Scripture richer and more instructive for faith and ministry than the interpretations that arise within any one of these circles alone.

THE OLD TESTAMENT CONTEXT OF PSALM 90

When considering the canonical context of a biblical text, it is important to understand that the status of the Old Testament as Scripture was a reality before the church existed. As theologian Robert Jenson states, ". . . the Old Testament and the New Testament are Scripture for the church in different ways. The Old Testament was Scripture for the apostles and other disciples before they were apostles and disciples."[93] As a result, it is necessary to deal with the Old Testament context of Psalm 90 separately before moving on to the context of the New Testament.

The common sense and critical sense readings of Psalm 90 reveal numerous literary connections between the psalm and the wider Old Testament. The most important of these connections for critical study proved to be the examples of communal prayers for help in Psalms and the immediate literary context of the end of Book III of the Psalms and the content of Book IV. Communal prayers for help show that the parts of Psalm 90 have a sense of unity, with a structure and flow to the psalm's argument. Sections of the psalm dealing with the brevity of life and the experience of divine wrath, rather than being primarily observations about human life in general, have specific functions within the prayers of postexilic Israel in particular. The remedy for this community's complaint is in the request expressed in v. 15: "Make us glad as many days as you have afflicted us, and as many years as we have seen evil."

The location of Psalm 90 within Book IV of the Psalms contextualizes it as a response to the anguished lament in Psalm 89 over the rejection of the dynasty and kingdom of David. Psalm 90 echoes words and themes found at the conclusion of Psalm 89:

> *How long, O LORD?* Will you hide your face forever? How long will *your wrath* burn like fire? Remember *how short my time is*—for what vanity *you have created all mortals!* Who can live and never see death? Who can escape the power of Sheol? Lord, where is *your steadfast love* of old, which by your faithfulness you swore to David? (vv. 46-49, emphasis added)

The themes of the lament at the end of Book III are taken up at the beginning of Book IV in the name of Moses, the exemplar of intercessory prayer in the Hebrew Scriptures. The figure of Moses is invoked numerous times in Book IV, primarily in association with prayer. Moses, Aaron, and Samuel are named in Psalm 99:6 as priestly intercessors *par excellence*. In Psalm 103, Moses is the mediator of the revelation of the LORD's gracious and merciful nature as one who abounds in steadfast love and does not hold his anger forever, but forgives the sins of his people because he remembers that they are dust (Ps 103:7-14). The final psalm in Book IV remembers that Moses saved Israel from God's decree of total judgment during the golden calf episode when he "stood in the breach before him, to turn away his wrath from destroying them" (Ps 106:23). Indeed, Psalms scholar Marvin Tate has described Book IV of the Psalms as "a Moses book."[94] Book IV, introduced by Psalm 90, directed the people's attention to a time before David when the Lord was the refuge of the people and when Moses interceded to turn away God's wrath and to reveal the promise that God's steadfast love is "from everlasting to everlasting" (Ps 103:17; cf. Ps 90:1-2).

The setting of Book IV locates Psalm 90 within the Old Testament traditions about Moses, particularly his roles as leader of the people, intercessor, and mediator of the covenant between God and Israel expressed in the Torah. Israel's long sojourn through the wilderness from slavery in Egypt to life in the promised land became the primary metaphor for Israel's self-understanding in the postexilic period. The Torah, the most authoritative and important Scripture in Judaism, ends with the people of Israel on the eastern side of the Jordan, waiting to enter the promised land. The Torah of Moses provided the body of instructions that the people were to follow in order to enter and thrive in the land. In the context of the Old Testament story of Moses, Psalm 90 becomes a part of God's instruction, or Torah, to the people of Israel. In the words of Samuel Balentine, "Moses' prayer belongs to this *torah*; in essence, Moses' words to God become God's words to successive generations of faithful travelers on the road from slavery to freedom."[95]

As words of Torah, Psalm 90 instructs the community to pray as Moses prayed during the golden calf episode in Exodus 32. In that story, while Moses was delayed on the mountain receiving the law of the covenant from God, the people in the camp gave up on Moses as their leader and requested an image of a god to lead them back to Egypt. Aaron made a golden calf idol that the people began to worship in what the biblical narrative describes as a festival of self-indulgent revelry (Exod 32:6). God reported the people's apostasy to Moses on the mountain and instructed Moses to leave God alone so that God could destroy the people in an act of complete judgment. Whatever the meaning of God's instruction to "leave me alone," Moses refused, offering a plaintive intercession on behalf of the people using the words of petition repeated in Ps 90:13: "Turn . . . and repent" (Exod 32:12 KJV). God listened to Moses' prayer and did not destroy the people as he had proposed to Moses.

As Moses' prayer in Exodus 32 was grounded in his faith in God's redeeming purpose anchored in the promises to Abraham and the exodus narrative, so the prayer in Psalm 90 is also grounded in convictions of faith about God's nature and God's purposes for the covenant people drawn from Israel's faith experience as depicted in the wider Old Testament canon. One such conviction is that God's compassion and steadfast love should prevail over wrath in response to the people's prayers. Another conviction alluded to in Psalm 90:11 is that the positive results of the people's response to God, "the fear of God," should not be eclipsed by the power of God's wrath.

As the pivotal lines in Psalm 90, vv. 11-12 contain a cluster of concepts that have deep roots in the broader canonical traditions about Moses. These concepts are the fear of God, the value of wisdom, and the use of time. Psalm 90 has important connections to the book of Deuteronomy, especially the Song of Moses in Deuteronomy 32 and the Blessing of Moses in Deuteronomy 33. The fear of God is an important theme in Deuteronomy. Moses exhorted the people in Deuteronomy 6:13, "The LORD your God you shall fear; him you shall serve, and by his name alone you shall swear." In this text and twelve others in the book, Moses instructs the people to fear the LORD by obeying the commandments of the covenant and by yielding exclusive allegiance to the LORD.[96]

The fear of God is often described as a source of wisdom for those who practice it. One of the most well-known statements about the fear of God and wisdom is Proverbs 1:7: "The fear of the LORD is the beginning of knowledge." Similar statements are found in Proverbs 3:7; 9:10; and 15:33, and in Job 28:28. This theme is not limited to the Wisdom corpus. It occurs in the Psalms (111:10) and the Prophets as well (Isa 11:2; 33:6; Mic 6:9). Since the book of Deuteronomy identifies the fear of God with obedience to the covenant, it is no surprise that it describes the covenant commandments as a source of wisdom also: "You must observe [the commandments] diligently, for this will show your wisdom and discernment to the peoples, who, when they hear all these statutes, will say, 'Surely this great nation is a wise and discerning people'" (Deut 4:6).

The proper use of time is a third theme in Psalm 90:11-12 that has associations with Moses and the covenant instructions connected to his ministry. McCann argues that the petitions of v. 12, "Teach us to count our days that we may gain a wise heart," and of v. 14, "Satisfy us in the morning with your steadfast love," should both be read in the context of the narrative of the giving of manna in Exodus 16.[97] When the people complained about their lack of food in the wilderness, God promised to give them "bread from heaven" in the form of manna to be gathered each morning, day by day. Embedded within the provision of manna was a command to gather the manna for six days but to rest from gathering on the seventh day, which was to be a "holy Sabbath to the LORD" (Exod 16:23). The provision of the manna becomes for the people a test to determine if they will obey the instruction (*torah*) of the LORD (Exod 16:4). It is also a form of discipline for nurturing Torah obedience. Numbering the days for gathering the manna was the way that the Israelites learned to obey the Torah during their allotted time in the wilderness. The themes of fear of God through Torah obedience, the wisdom of the divine instructions, and the proper use of time come together in the narrative of the gathering of the manna and in the instructions to obey the Sabbath command.

In Psalm 90:11, the writer complains that the unrelenting wrath of God threatens to nullify the people's proper fear of God, that is, their proper obedience to God's will revealed through Torah. If God were to temper divine wrath in response to this prayer, the result would enable God's servants to number their days rightly. In enabling the people's obedience to Torah, exemplified in observance of the Sabbath, by turning from wrath, God would indeed allow them to gain the wisdom that has its beginning in the fear of the LORD.

By locating the psalm within the tradition of Moses, Psalm 90 addresses the topics of the brevity of life and the gulf between God's eternality and human transience in a way that is different from the treatment of these topics in Israel's wisdom tradition. Like Psalm 90, the book of Job is also a lament of one whose days are consumed by wrath:

A mortal, born of woman, few of days and full of trouble, comes up like a flower and withers, flees like a shadow and does not last. . . . The waters wear away the stones; the torrents wash away the soil of the earth; so you destroy the hope of mortals. You prevail forever against them, and they pass away. (Job 14:1-2, 19-20)

Likewise, Ecclesiastes bemoaned the brevity of life with no discernible connection between one's conduct and circumstances: "For who knows what is good for mortals while they live the few days of their vain life, which they pass like a shadow? For who can tell what will be after them under the sun?" (Eccl 6:12). While Job protested his innocence and demanded vindication, Ecclesiastes made no petitions at all, concluding that God was too far removed to respond to human pleas. "Never be rash with your mouth," the author wrote, "nor let your heart be quick to utter a word before God, for God is in heaven, and you upon earth; therefore let your words be few" (Eccl 5:2). Psalm 90, though confessing that the cause of God's wrath was human iniquity, protested indefinite punishment out of the conviction that the fear of God ought to result in wisdom and its attendant blessings. This affirmation distinguished the Mosaic tradition from that of the sages and foreshadowed a synthesis of Torah and wisdom in post-biblical literature.

The title "the prayer of Moses" and the setting of Book IV of the Psalms provide Psalm 90 with important connections to the Old Testament story. The psalm directs the praying community to the age of Moses, a time when God ruled Israel directly, delivering them and guiding them on their wilderness journey. Moses was the mediator of God's covenant with Israel, making God's character and will known to them. The covenant was the basis for Moses' exemplary prayers of intercession and also the grounds for the people's confidence that their fear of God in the form of Torah obedience would yield wisdom and life to them.

THE NEW TESTAMENT CONTEXT OF PSALM 90

The New Testament alludes to Psalm 90 in only one text. Recalling Psalm 90:4, 2 Peter 3:8 reminds its readers that "with the Lord one day is like a thousand years, and a thousand years are like one day." In Psalm 90, the description of God's time perspective is part of the motivation for the petitions of vv. 13-17. Because human life is brief, prolonged wrath is a serious threat. Second Peter invokes the description of the difference between divine and human perceptions of time as a defense against skeptics who point to the delay of Christ's return as a reason to dismiss Christian faith. In both cases, the problem is caused by a delay. In Psalm 90, it is a delay in the end of the community's experience of wrath. In 2 Peter, it is a delay in the anticipated return of Christ. Psalm 90:4 supports the urgency of the psalm's petitions by emphasizing that human life is too short to endure unrelenting wrath. In 2 Peter 3, the differing perspectives serve an apologetic function. God's time frame cannot be evaluated by human perceptions of time. Further, any perceived delay is evidence of God's mercy in allowing more time for repentance (2 Pet 3:9).

It is perhaps surprising that the New Testament does not contain formal examples of corporate prayers for help similar to the prayer in Psalm 90. Acts 4:23-31 is an example of a corporate prayer of the church following the arrest and release of Peter and John. The prayer does contain a petition for boldness in announcing the gospel in the face of persecution. It does not, however, contain an explicit element of complaint similar to corporate prayers for help in the Psalms. The fact that corporate laments are not recorded in the New Testament, however, does not mean that such prayers were not a part of early Christian worship. Acts 8 reports that devout men buried Stephen following his execution and "made loud lamentation over him" (Acts 8:2). In Acts 12:5, the church prays fervently for Peter during his imprisonment following the martyrdom of James. There are numerous references to corporate prayer in the New Testament. In his comprehensive study of biblical prayer, Patrick Miller argued that there was a high degree of continuity between the prayers of the early Christians and the prayers of the Jewish Scriptures and the tradition of prayer that developed in early Judaism.[98] There is ample evidence that the early Christians retained the prayers of the Psalms and early Jewish liturgy and adapted those prayers to their own needs and circumstances.

Psalm 90 and the Lord's Prayer

The primary example of a corporate prayer in the New Testament that functioned similarly to Psalm 90 as an instructional guide to prayer is the Lord's Prayer recorded in Matthew 6:9-13 and Luke 11:2-4. The prayer of Moses in Psalm 90 is a model for communal prayer for the postexilic community just as the Lord's Prayer is a model prayer for the Christian community. The Lord's Prayer does not explicitly contain the formal elements of the communal prayer of lament, although some of these elements are implicit within the prayer. It does not offer a protest, as the Old Testament corporate laments do, of a perceived gap between what the community has been taught to expect and what they are currently experiencing. However, the petition "your kingdom come, your will be done on earth as it is in heaven" does acknowledge a gap between God's will and what the community currently experiences "on earth." Also, a subtle element of motivation is found in the structure of the Lord's Prayer. In the initial part of the prayer, the community commits itself completely to the cause of God's name, God's kingdom, and God's will. On the basis of this commitment, the prayer proceeds to ask for God's commitment to the community in the form of daily provision, forgiveness, guidance, and deliverance.

Though Psalm 90 and the Lord's Prayer differ regarding the formal elements of the corporate lament, both prayers begin with a statement of praise and submission to God as lord and sovereign. Psalm 90 acknowledges God as a refuge in generations past and as eternal creator. The Lord's Prayer addresses God as a heavenly father and pledges commitment to the sanctification of God's name among all peoples. The Lord's Prayer both affirms and intensifies the metaphor of God as the dwelling place or home in Psalm 90 by addressing God as "our Father." God is not only the true home of God's servants but also the providential patron of the household who embraces and adopts his servants as children within God's own family.

Psalm 90 and the Lord's Prayer are also alike in containing multiple petitions. Like Psalm 90, the Lord's Prayer makes an apparent allusion to the story of the manna in the wilderness in its petition for "daily bread." The prayer of Psalm 90:14, "satisfy us in the morning with your steadfast love," is a suggestive parallel to the petition "give us this day our daily bread." It is often observed that New Testament prayers tend to spiritualize needs that in the Old Testament are presented as concrete and tangible. Interestingly, in this case it is the Old Testament text that requests a spiritual benefit, steadfast love, and the New Testament text that requests the physical benefit of daily bread. Both Psalm 90 and the Lord's Prayer also acknowledge the condition of sin and the need for forgiveness. Psalm 90:8 acknowledges that the community's iniquity is exposed in the light of God's presence. Psalm 90:13-14 asks for God's compassion and mercy. Though the words of the Lord's Prayer do not lament a specific problem like that of prolonged wrath in Psalm 90, they do acknowledge that periods of trial like that lamented in Psalm 90 are a possibility. Those who say this prayer therefore seek relief from such trials in advance. The petition "deliver us from evil" provides a general request for divine help with threats and troubles of various kinds. These parallels between Psalm 90 and the Lord's Prayer illustrate a spiritual tradition cited by Dietrich Bonhoeffer that sees the petitions of the Lord's Prayer as condensed expressions of the petitions in the Psalms.[99]

Prayer in the New Testament

Although prayer in the New Testament shows much continuity with the prayers of the Old Testament and Jewish piety, Miller identified features of early Christian prayer that distinguished it from its Old Testament and Jewish sources. One is that the New Testament contains more instruction about prayer than the Old Testament does. The manner in which a community prayed was something that distinguished one religious community from another. One of the features of New Testament instruction is its teaching about persistent, constant prayer as a spiritual discipline.[100] Psalm 90 represents a community that prays for divine compassion through a long period of suffering. In this way it serves as an intrinsic model for the extrinsic teaching on persistent prayer in the New Testament.

Another difference in New Testament prayers relates to the element of motivation to help that is a frequent feature of Old Testament laments. Old Testament prayers often ground their petitions with arguments that the requests are in keeping with both the nature and the interests of God. The shorthand version of this argument is the phrase "for your name's sake."[101] The request made "for your name's sake" is a request in line with the character, will, and purpose of God in extending the revelation of God's name and nature to the nations. Miller observed that many New Testament prayers subordinate the request for help and the supporting arguments for their fulfillment to a greater desire for God's will to be done.[102] Miller connected this change in the form of New Testament prayer to the core Christian convictions about the significance of Jesus' crucifixion and resurrection. In the cross, Jesus' suffering became a means of redemption for others. The transformation of the injustice of Jesus' death into a salvific event gave New Testament prayer an openness to the possibility that suffering could fulfill a redemptive purpose. Jesus' prayer in the Garden of Gethsemane, "Not my will, but yours be done," transferred the emphasis in New Testament prayer from petitions for one's own deliverance to intercession for others, even at the cost of self-sacrifice (Lk 22:42). As a prayer attributed to Moses, Psalm 90 recalls key moments of Moses' intercessory prayers on behalf of Israel. In New Testament prayer, such intercession for others becomes a role and an expectation not just for leaders but also for the entire Christian community.[103]

Although the New Testament makes explicit reference to Psalm 90 only once, the general pattern of prayer in the New Testament continues the pattern of prayer demonstrated in this psalm. Psalm 90 models prayer in many ways that are similar to the model prayer that Jesus gave to the Christian community. New Testament teaching on prayer emphasizes that prayer in the spirit of Psalm 90 should be persistent to the point of becoming an essential spiritual discipline. The redemptive purpose of the cross in the mystery of Jesus' work of salvation, however, suggested to Christians that prayers for help such as Psalm 90 should be offered for more than one's own community. The New Testament's emphasis on intercession as the work of the entire community, however, is foreshadowed in the communal nature of the prayer in Psalm 90.

HIGHLIGHTS OF THE HISTORY OF CHRISTIAN EXEGESIS OF PSALM 90

Identifying what Gabriel Fackre called the canonical sense of the text was the primary goal of Christian teachers and theologians who studied and taught before the advent of secular, academic study of the Bible. These scholars and teachers read the Scriptures of the Old and New Testaments as one interwoven tapestry whose ultimate content was the revelation of the triune God of Christian worship. Although the history of exegesis before the rise of the historical-critical approach is often called "precritical exegesis," this is a misnomer. Exegesis before the time of historical-critical studies was highly sophisticated, versed in the best linguistic and historical knowledge of the time, and sensitive to phenomena in the text that raised questions for both sympathetic and skeptical readers alike.[104] The examples below are intended to suggest ways that theological convictions can serve as a guide rather than a hindrance to biblical interpretation.

Patristic Interpretation

An example of awareness of critical issues on the part of ancient interpreters can be seen in the question of the authorship of Psalm 90. Despite the attribution to Moses in v. 1, patristic teachers like Clement of Alexandria (d. 215) and Athanasius (d. 373) attributed the psalm, like much of the rest of the Psalter, to David.[105]

The same question about authorship can be seen in the interpretation of Psalm 90 by Augustine of Hippo (d. 430), perhaps the greatest theologian of the patristic era, in an exposition of the psalm in its entirety.[106] He described the words "the prayer of Moses" as a title intended not as a statement of authorship but rather as a clue to the reader of the psalm. Like the master of classical rhetoric that he was, Augustine saved his explanation of this clue for the end of his exposition. For him, the key to the message of the psalm was the contrast between the eternal life of God and the temporal life of human beings. Using the Greek translation, Augustine took the divine decree in v. 3, "turn back, you mortals," as an exhortation to humanity to turn away from temporal desires and to make eternity their primary concern. Again, reading with the Greek translation, he read the phrase in v. 12, "You make known your right hand," as a promise fulfilled in Christ. In Christ, the eternal and the temporal are found together, and, as a result of the incarnation, revelation is given for people to enable them to pass over from the earthly to the eternal realm. For Augustine, the title "a prayer of Moses" was a sign to the reader that, like this psalm, the Torah of Moses also looks beyond temporal, earthly rewards only and makes a veiled but discernible witness to the eternal hope revealed through Christ.[107]

Augustine's comment that the Torah, like Psalm 90, contains deeper meanings about eternal life shows that early Christian interpreters held the Old Testament in high esteem, though they interpreted it in relation to their understanding of the centrality of the Christ event. The impetus to look for greater meaning in addition to the literal, historically grounded meaning of the text can be seen in Augustine's interpretation of Ps 90:10. He dismissed the idea that the statement "the days of our life are seventy years or perhaps eighty if we are strong" was a literal description of the human life span. Some people would have lived longer in antiquity, while many would have died earlier than age 70. If the statement is not to be read literally, then Augustine concluded it should be read "spiritually" or symbolically, according to the practices of his time. He treated the numbers seventy and eighty as variants of the numbers seven and eight. Seven symbolized completion and eight symbolized something new and beyond the ordinary. Seven was the number of the days of creation and of the Sabbath as its completion, while eight was the number of the day of resurrection and of new creation. Just as the resurrection includes and transforms the Sabbath, for Augustine Christian faith includes and transforms the literal sense of the Jewish Scriptures in light of the revelation received through Christ.

The sense that Augustine's interpretation was a standard Christian way of reading Psalm 90 and not an idiosyncratic one is confirmed by the comments of his contemporary Jerome (d. 420). Like Augustine, he read the words "Turn back, O mortals" of v. 3 as a call to repentance, and he interpreted the words "right hand" of v. 12 as a reference to Christ. He also offered a spiritual interpretation for the numbers seventy and eighty in v. 10. Like Augustine, the primary message of the psalm was to turn away from temporal concerns and focus on the promise of eternal life that is

God's gift through Christ. Augustine and Jerome give witness to a shared Christian tradition of interpretation of Psalm 90 in the patristic period.[108]

In general, patristic interpreters focused on the broad contrasts in the psalm between God and humanity and between earthly life and eternal life. They did not deny that the psalm was rooted in the historical particularity of God's revelation to Israel. Gregory of Nyssa, for example, characterized the psalm's message of the contrast between human weakness and divine power as the central struggle in the narrative of Moses' life, therefore making Moses the perfect teacher representing God to humanity and the perfect intercessor representing humanity before God.[109] The particular, historical elements of Israel's history and Scripture, however, were themselves imbued with a larger message addressed to all humanity. In these scholars' eyes, the incarnation, death, and resurrection of Jesus transformed the revelation given to Israel into a message for all humanity.

Reformation Interpretation: Luther and Calvin

Augustine's exposition of Psalm 90 described its message using the broad categories of eternal versus earthly concerns. Luther also highlighted a basic duality in the psalm's message. He described its content, however, in relation to the twin dualities of divine wrath and divine grace on the one hand, and death versus eternal life on the other.[110] The content of the psalm, according to Luther, was consumed by a burden to demonstrate the reality of God's wrath toward hardened and smug sinners who do not give thought to the inevitability of their own death and so do not understand that their death is an expression of the wrath of God toward sin. Luther's interpretation combined the theme of vv. 3-6, the brevity of life, with the theme of vv. 7-10, God's wrath. For Luther, "the wrath of God" was not a description of a community calamity or a punishment for sin through the vehicle of historical forces. Accepting v. 1 as a statement of authorship (contrary to Augustine), he interpreted the wrath of God as Moses' expression for the reality of death and its theological cause. Luther described Psalm 90 as typical of Moses' office as a minister of the Law and therefore as a minister of death, wrath, and sin. For Luther, the psalm showed "Moses at his most Mosaic."[111] The purpose of the psalm was to reveal the truth of God's wrath at work in the brevity and trouble of life, and in the reality and tragic nature of death. This revelation serves a purpose similar to the purpose of the Mosaic Law, which is to reveal to humanity its sinful nature so that they will turn in faith to God for mercy. Luther wrote, "Moses informs us that life is not a span of time, but it is, as it were, a violent toss which catapults us into death."[112] This revelation was necessary because a worse misfortune than being condemned to death would be ignorance of one's true standing before God. For Luther, this is the meaning of v. 11, "Who knows the power of your wrath?" Luther ignored the communal form of the prayer and read it as Moses praying alone as the teacher of Israel. The lament of divine wrath in vv. 7-10 was not the complaint of the community but the instruction of their teacher, Moses. The masses, according Luther, do not understand their own condition.

Although Luther saw the content of the psalm to be about the terror of death as an expression of divine wrath, the form of the psalm as a prayer was a hint that the condemned may find hope and mercy in seeking God. For Luther, the act of prayer was always an act of hope. He used Jesus' statement in Matthew 24:22 that God is not the God of the dead but the God of the living as evidence of a hermeneutical principle that whenever Scripture discusses matters of worship, faith, or prayer, it points to the hope of the resurrection. The purpose of the psalm, like the purpose of the Law, was to convince sinful people of their utter need for divine mercy. The turning point in the psalm is v. 12, which Luther understood as a prayer that God would give people the knowledge that they will die under the condemnation of God's wrath so that they can order their lives before God rightly and wisely.[113] This knowledge alone can prepare people to seek God's mercy revealed in the eternal life offered by Christ. According to Luther, the petitions in vv. 13-17 were Moses' prayer for the few, humble servants of God who accept their judgment for sin and put their hope in God for eternal life beyond death. In vv. 13-17, Moses gave a prophecy, as it were, of the gospel to be proclaimed by Jesus and his apostles.[114] Psalm 90 was thus an example of Luther's theology of law and gospel in miniature.

The Old Testament context of Psalm 90 focused on the meaning of the prayer for the people of Israel and on the role of Moses as intercessor and teacher of the community. The narrative background of the wilderness sojourn and its application in the postexilic period were the primary contexts of interpretation. Luther's interpretation focused on Moses as mediator and symbol of the Old Testament Law in terms described by Paul in the New Testament. The Law was given to reveal sin and to demonstrate the need for grace. The addressees of the psalm were not the descendants of Israel but rather the universal descendants of Adam and Eve who share in the consequences of the fall. The wrath of God, which in the Old Testament context was a temporal experience of righteous judgment to be endured by the covenant community, was in Luther's reading a universal condition similar to Paul's description of God's wrath in Romans 1–2. For Luther, Psalm 90 was not a prayer of the worshiping community. He saw the elements of complaint in vv. 7-10 as temptations to blasphemy that are not to be imitated. They serve primarily as an example of how Moses dealt with such thoughts by resisting them and remaining anchored in faith.[115] The psalm was the prayer of Moses the Lawgiver who taught in the form of this one prayer the lesson of the Law in general about sin, death, and the need for grace.

John Calvin's exposition of Psalm 90 combined themes identified by Augustine and Luther while adding elements unique to his own theological position.[116] With Luther, he expressed the psalm's description of life under God's wrath as a wretched condition, while with Augustine, he identified the chief characteristic of the condemned as "allowing their hearts to rest in the world." Illustrative of the role that the judicial metaphor played in Calvin's theology, he identified the primary difficulty that the objects of God's wrath face to be their indifference to the fact that "God summons them as guilty sinners to his judgment seat."

Regarding the title of the psalm, with Luther he left behind the patristic tendency to associate the entire Psalter with David. However, he also showed an awareness of critical views of Mosaic authorship. He accepted the possibility that a scribe could have assembled Mosaic quotes or fragments into a complete prayer, but he personally had no doubts that Moses was the author. He pointed to the description in v. 15 of the "many years as we have seen evil" as evidence that the psalm was written in the wilderness near the end of Moses' life.

Calvin described the psalm as a refutation of the conceit that a person's life goes on forever without being called into account before the heavenly Judge. He interpreted v. 11, "Who considers the power of your anger?" as a description of self-deception rather than a lack of knowledge. In a rhetorical flourish, he lamented that humans can "number the feet from the moon to the center of the earth, the space between the planets, the dimensions of heaven and earth," but cannot count the limited days of their own lives. He explained the difficult second line of v. 11, "according to your fear is your wrath," to mean that only the humble who fear God and acknowledge God's righteous judgment perceive the reality of divine wrath. Those who should fear God's wrath the least are the ones most sensitive to its possibility. Only those who rightly understand the end of life will consider that its purpose is to secure the prize of life after death. Since

Moses perceived that the great majority of people cannot understand this truth without divine illumination, he made this knowledge a matter of prayer. Aware that God's wrath is described in the Old Testament as God turning away from his people, the petition for God to turn back in v. 13 was explained as seeking God's favor. Though Calvin described punishment as no less a part of God's work than mercy, the mercy sought in vv. 13-17 was, in his view, God's "most natural work." The petition in v. 16 that the "beauty and splendor" of God be revealed to the people speaks to God's most characteristic desire, which is to do good to God's creatures.

For Calvin, the psalm was a meditation on the human heart that is alienated from a proper understanding of one's relationship to God as creator, sovereign, and judge. The description of this condition is as dire as Luther's description, but the tone is more pastoral. The heart of the prayer in Calvin's view was the petition in v. 12 that people be given knowledge to understand their true condition in life, with the result that they would seek God's mercy as subjects and servants.

This sampling of interpreters from patristic and Reformation history shows a high value for the Old Testament on the part of Christian teachers in premodern times. They did not approach Old Testament texts in isolation, however, but instead recontextualized them in light of the revelation of God made known in Jesus and handed down through the apostles and evangelists of the New Testament. Each interpreter also brought the influence of his own theological programs to his interpretation of the text. Augustine read Psalm 90 in light of his philosophical understanding of God as eternal and the true source of life and blessing. Luther saw within the psalm the essential elements of his theology of law and grace. Calvin interpreted it through the lens of the concept of divine justice. None of these teachers ignored the Old Testament context of the psalm. For them, however, the broader contexts of the New Testament and of Christian faith were the ultimate and guiding contexts for interpretation.

THE CONTRIBUTION OF CREEDS AND CONFESSIONS

Fackre's description of the canonical sense of the text included not only the setting of the entire canon and the exegesis of the church's theologians but also the contribution of a congregation's creedal and confessional tradition.[117] The historical, ecumenical creeds are primarily summaries of the Bible's grand narrative that describe the gospel story in its basic elements. Fackre described Scripture as the source of the Christian message and the summaries of church tradition in the creeds as a resource for understanding Scripture properly. He also affirmed the classical theological distinction between the Spirit's inspiration of Scripture and the Spirit's illumination of the church that is preserved in its tradition. The fact that the ecumenical creeds omit both the story of Israel and the events of Jesus' earthly life remind the interpreter, however, that the creeds are guides to interpretation that always require expansion and correction based on the text and substance of Scripture itself.[118]

For the purposes of this study, I will use the Apostle's Creed as a resource for examining the canonical sense of Psalm 90. One benefit of viewing the psalm through the lens of this creed is that it provides clarification of the differences between the critical sense of the psalm and the interpretations found in patristic and Reformation commentators described above. The impact of the Christian message as summarized in the Apostle's Creed helps to explain why Christian theologians emphasized different aspects of the psalm than the ones that stand out within the Old Testament context alone. The creedal context of the psalm can also point out the benefits of listening to both the Old Testament context and the broader context of Christian confessional traditions.

The Apostle's Creed begins with an affirmation of "God the Father, Almighty, creator of heaven and earth." Although it uses different language, Psalm 90 also begins with an affirmation of God as the almighty creator who exercises sovereignty over not only God's chosen people but also "the earth and the world" (v. 2). Although the psalm does not use the title of Father, the affirmation of God as the dwelling place of God's people suggests that as the people's true "home," God's relationship with them has positive, familial overtones that are consistent with the imagery connoted by the name Father. This affirmation of God is the primary point of orientation for the psalm's pleas for God's justice, wisdom, and mercy. As eternal creator, God is not limited by the time constraints that define humans as finite creatures. This places the praying community entirely at the mercy of God's self-determined timing of redemption. As sovereign ruler, God brings secret sins to light (v. 8). As a result, God is just in condemning and limiting sin, both that of the covenant community and that of the human family in general.

While Psalm 90 aligns well with the Apostle's Creed's affirmation of "God the Father Almighty, Creator of heaven and earth," the psalm also affirms aspects of God's character that are central to the story of Israel yet omitted from direct expression in the creed. The psalm appeals to characteristics of mercy, faithfulness, and justice in God that resist letting judgment and wrath be the final word in God's dealings with people. There is an assumption that the fear of God should have a mitigating effect on the wrath of God (v. 11). These assumptions about God's character are dependent on the primary Old Testament tradition of the exodus as a demonstration of God's justice, mercy, and faithfulness to the covenant people, epitomized in the life and ministry of Moses. Elements of the revelation of God's character to Israel contributed to the portrayal of God as Father in both canon and creed. God is addressed or described as a father in several Old Testament texts (Ps 68:5 and 103:13; Prov 3:12; Isa 63:16 and 64:8; Jer 3:4, 19 and 31:9; and Mal 1:6). Psalm 90, however, makes explicit the qualities of God's character as Father that are at best implicit in the creed.

The second article of the Apostle's Creed confesses faith in "Jesus Christ, his only Son our Lord" and briefly narrates key elements of his story: his conception, virgin birth, passion, death, resurrection, ascension, and return. Clearly, in its Old Testament context, Psalm 90 does not refer to the events of Jesus' life and their significance. Having said that, however, the Christ event is central in the Christian message and transforms the way Christians view God, the world, and humanity. This transformation also affects the way Christians view the Old Testament Scripture that preceded the life of Jesus, including Psalm 90. This transformation is evident in the examples of ancient Christian exegesis discussed above. The comparison in v. 6, for example, between human life and grass, drew Augustine's attention to a similar statement in Isa 40:6 that "all people are grass." This brought to mind for him the wonder of the incarnation that the eternal Son would take on mortal human flesh that by its very definition as flesh was destined to die.[119] Both Augustine and Jerome commented on the Greek text of v. 12, which reads "make known your right hand," instead of the Hebrew reading "make [us] know how to count our days." They asserted that God has made his right hand known in the person of Jesus Christ. The prayer of v. 12 as it was passed down in the Greek translation was answered in Christian understanding in the revelation of Jesus as the Son of God.[120]

The faith story outlined in Christian ecumenical creeds has influenced not only Christian interpretations of individual elements of Psalm 90 but also the understanding of the psalm as a whole. The psalm in its Old Testament context is a plea for divine mercy in the temporal realm. It is a model of how to pray boldly, praying, as it were, "to God against God." It is also an affirmation of the wisdom of Israel's Torah as a helpful guide in navigating the interim between the prayer for help and the experience of divine mercy. In Christian interpretation, on the other hand, the psalm is a didactic prayer that teaches its hearers to value eternal life and communion with God above earthly, time-bound concerns. The perspective of the broad Christian story of the eternal God breaking into history to rescue humanity from sin and death broadens the perspective of the psalm from concern about life under unrelenting judgment to concern for embracing the eternal life made known in the resurrection of Jesus. In the Christian interpretations of the patristic and Reformation periods surveyed above, the creedal affirmations of the forgiveness of sins, the resurrection of the body, and life everlasting give further definition to the theme of eternal life perceived in the language of the psalm.

Although the Old Testament context and the Christian canonical and creedal contexts differ in their understanding of the primary form and message of the psalm, both perspectives agree in seeing a message of hope that underlies the psalm's content. In the Old Testament context, the hope is grounded in the covenantal character of God revealed in God's dealings with Moses and summarized by the Hebrew word *hesed*, a term rendered variously as steadfast love, tender mercy, and loving kindness. The term has the general meaning of "covenantal faithfulness." In the Christian creedal context, hope lies in the gracious character of God revealed most fully in the benevolent life, vicarious death, and triumphal resurrection of Jesus, a revelation of the life that believers experience by faith in the future unfolding of God's redemptive work. In both readings, a present trouble is met with a future hope that strengthens and guides the believing community.

CONCLUSION: BENEFITS OF THE CANONICAL SENSE OF THE TEXT

It is possible to see the differing interpretations of Psalm 90 found in the Old Testament context, the New Testament context, and the Christian confessional context as being in conflict with one another and therefore as evidence that either the religious reading or the critical reading must be the superior one. This conclusion, however, is neither necessary nor preferable. An alternative to this conclusion is to see each interpretation as embedded within a particular context and to appreciate the value that multiple contexts and perspectives present to readers of this psalm and to readers of the Bible in general. The Old Testament, New Testament, and confessional interpretations set the psalm within the framework of particular theologies. The Old Testament contextual theology was concerned with the identity and security of the worshiping community of Israel in relation to God. Since its circumstances were dire enough to threaten the continued coherence of their faith, the complaints and petitions of Psalm 90 were urgently and boldly stated. The New Testament context shared some continuity with this form of communal prayer, but it also discerned a new awareness that in the Christ event the community received a broader horizon for understanding and coping with the experiences of suffering and transience. Patristic commentators shared the New Testament's perspective and broadened the context of interpretation to include the larger narrative of the Bible's story of redemption from creation to new creation. The Reformation interpreters Luther and Calvin shared the creedal theology of patristic teachers while also incorporating their own theological perspectives. Luther interpreted the psalm within his theology of law and gospel, while Calvin emphasized the centrality of understanding God as righteous judge and gracious savior.

Fackre described the canonical sense of the text as the way the text works to proclaim the gospel message made known in Christ. The Christian interpretations of Psalm 90 address this specific, and important, level of meaning. The Old Testament contextual meaning, however, also contributes to the canonical sense. It provides a model of prayer for a community under duress. It points to the Torah as a source of wisdom for the worshiping community and looks to disciplined obedience as a grounds for hope for the community. It provides language that Christian communities of intercession can use to pray for their own needs and for the needs of others. Psalm 90 is an example of what Frederick Holmgren has referred to as the "plus" of the Old Testament.[121] The Old Testament canon addresses issues and life situations that do not receive attention in the New Testament's focus on the priority of the Christ event. This diversity of experience informs and enriches Christian faith, as attested by the efforts of ancient interpreters to plumb the depths of the text's meaning.

Each of the theological contexts of Psalm 90 is important and beneficial. There is a necessity to pray with the boldness of Moses for communities that are oppressed and imperiled to such a degree that it challenges faith in the justice and goodness of God. Such prayers are not completely absent within the New Testament, but the New Testament writers add a perception that the understanding of suffering and injustice needs to be framed within the witness of the cross. Patristic and Reformation interpretations add additional theological perspectives and also provide models of spiritual illumination and theological contextualization.

The contemporary world of biblical interpretation is an increasingly complex and pluralistic context composed of many overlapping and competing frameworks of understanding. The Christian canonical sense of the text prepares readers for the work of contextualization by laying out some of the multiple contexts present within the Christian tradition. The work of contextualizing the message of Psalm 90 in the setting of the contemporary world defines the task for the next step of theological interpretation, the contextual sense of the text.

Chapter 6

The Contextual Sense of the Text: A Conversation with the World

"A biblical text reaches its destination when it is appropriated in context."[122] This statement by Gabriel Fackre expresses the ultimate role of application in the process of biblical interpretation. The Bible shapes, influences, and guides individuals and communities in their thoughts, actions, habits, and character in ways that impact people and communities. In theological terms, the Spirit's work of inspiration in the creation of the biblical text is complemented by the Spirit's work of illumination in the lives of its readers. Fackre refers to this fourth level of theological interpretation as the contextual sense of the text. The contextual sense is the result of the revealed truth for all becoming "truth for us" in the social context and "truth for me" in the personal context.[123]

The necessity of contextualization and application of Scripture does not diminish in the least the complexity of this step in the interpretive process. Biblical texts are not self-explanatory or self-actualizing. On the one hand, the illuminating presence of the Holy Spirit assists the church in allowing the inspired, written word to become flesh in the lives, hearts, and actions of reading communities. On the other hand, the challenge of moving from written text to contemporary context is fraught with complexity and possibilities for error. Not the least of the challenges is the fact that while the text is found in the church, the church lives in a fallen world. Moreover, the fallenness and resistance to God that exists in the world also inhabits and inhibits the church.

The task of clarifying the content and meaning of the biblical text is referred to as the task of *exegesis*, while the task of appropriating the meaning is labeled *hermeneutics*. The distinction suggests that contextualization is a separate discipline of study, one with its own theories, methodologies, and orthodoxies. Admittedly, more is involved in applying the biblical text to contemporary life than mimicking biblical actions and attitudes. Theories of hermeneutics, especially when applied in concrete examples of interpretation, are beneficial for interpreting the Bible responsibly. A strong distinction between exegesis and hermeneutics, however, can also be a discouragement to confident interpretation. If specialists are required to master sophisticated theoretical procedures and adhere to careful disciplinary boundaries in moving from text to interpretation, how can the individual pastor with limited time and resources, or the committed disciple or lay teacher, be expected to bridge with confidence the gap between the biblical then and the contextual now? While respecting the value and contribution of philosophical hermeneutics, my approach to contextualizing Psalm 90 for contemporary faith and practice admittedly employs a broad and flexible concept of hermeneutics.[124]

MODELS OF CONTEXTUALIZATION

As a "pastoral systematics" aimed at assisting the congregational minister in the regular exercise of pastoral ministry, Fackre's guidelines for addressing the contextual sense of the text engage with the nuances of hermeneutical theory while presenting models that are accessible enough for the generalist role required of pastoral ministry. He described four models of contextualization that provide an inclusive scope for congregationally based theological interpretation.

Contextualization as Translation

Translation is the model of contextualization that maintains the closest relationship to the text of Scripture.[125] The process of linguistic translation serves as a metaphor for theological translation of concepts from the biblical text to contemporary contexts. The goal is an expression of the biblical meaning in contemporary thought, values, and actions. Fackre described three modes of translation-based contextualization. (1) *Literal translation* is effectively a search to find contemporary synonyms for the biblical wording. It puts the burden on the receiving culture to conform to the concepts and constructs of the biblical text. (2) *Paraphrase* is the form of translation that exercises the greatest degree of freedom toward the biblical text, giving primary emphasis to issues and concerns in the contemporary context. (3) Fackre described the *dynamic equivalence model* of translation as the ideal approach to contextualization, preserving the integrity of biblical meaning in contemporary forms of action that faithfully express the content of the text.

In Psalm 90, an example of contextualization as translation is found in the interpretation of the wrath/anger of God. The wrath of God is the dominant theme in vv. 7-11. An example of literal translation of this concept is found in Luther's and Calvin's interpretations. They describe the wrath of God not as a human emotion stretched to describe an aspect of the divine but rather as a divine emotion that rages against human sin. The wrath of God is similar to the human emotion of wrath, only exponentially more powerful and more threatening. Translation of the wrath of God in the mode of paraphrase is best illustrated by the treatment of Psalm 90 in contemporary lectionaries that set forth Scripture readings for weekly worship on a three-year reading cycle. The *Revised Common Lectionary*, the most widely used lectionary in mainline Protestant churches, recommends omitting vv. 7-11, which mention God's wrath, or vv. 9-11, the strongest description of divine wrath ("who comprehends the power of your anger?" [v. 11]), from the public reading of Psalm 90.[126] This approach deals with the negative connotations of associating harmful or violent emotions with God, but it comes at the cost of diminishing the concreteness and otherness of Scripture. Critical scholars and theologians tend to follow a model of dynamic equivalence. They describe wrath as biblical language for God's righteous opposition to human autonomy. It is language borrowed from human experience to describe God's response to human opposition to God's will. James L. Mays is a good example. He writes that divine wrath is "a linguistic symbol for the divine limits and pressure placed against human resistance to [God's] sovereignty."[127]

In contrast to the language of the wrath of God in Psalm 90, the meaning of Ps 90:12 is rarely described by interpreters according to its literal sense. The language of v. 12, "teach us to count our days that we may gain a wise heart," has the sense of a riddle about it, apparently pointing to something beyond the literal words. Luther, who spoke quite literally about the wrath of God, comes closer to the model of paraphrase in his description of v. 12: "Teach us to reflect on the fact that we must die, so that we become wise."[128] Weiser described v. 12 as a prayer for a new valuation and appreciation of the life that is described in dark terms in v. 10 as full of toil and trouble.[129] Clifford's historical-critical exegesis yielded a more literal interpretation. According to his interpretation, the problem addressed in vv. 11-12 was not a lack of understanding of the reality of divine wrath or the brevity of life but rather the indefinite duration of judgment. The psalm is a complaint about wrath that has no apparent end. In that situation, v. 12 asks for a remedy: "Let us know how to compute accurately our days (of affliction) so that we may bring wisdom (into) our minds."[130] Even this more literal interpretation requires some further elaboration in order to be meaningful. Knowing the number of days of wrath is meaningful in the sense of having assurance that the period of wrath will come to an end. The assurance of an ending, rather than the number of days to compute, would be the crux of this prayer.

The interpretation of v. 12 that moves farthest from the language of the text in order to express the contextual significance may be that of Balentine, who considers the function of v. 12 in the overall structure of the psalm and in the broader Old Testament tradition of lament. Verses 1-11 voice a prayer of lament from the perspective of the general human experience of wrath, judgment, and calamity. Verses 13-17 voice a powerful series of petitions inspired by Moses' prayer for divine repentance during the episode of the golden calf. The significance of v. 12, Balentine argued, lies in its request for wisdom about how to pray. Should the worshiping community accept its brief life of suffering with resignation and lament, as expressed in vv. 3-10, or should it give voice to hope and pray like Moses and other servants of God do in vv. 13-17?[131] This is the wisdom the prayer requests. This interpretation demonstrates the greatest freedom in departing from the wording of the text, but it also captures well the psalm's implications about the role and meaning of prayer.

As argued in the critical examination of the psalm, I propose a reading of v. 11 in line with the Greek translation as a question primarily of theodicy: "Who knows the power of your anger, or whether your wrath is greater than the fear of you?" An indefinite experience of wrath and suffering would render the virtue of the fear of God meaningless. Similar to the interpretation of Balentine, this translation shows v. 12 to be a plea for God to answer the question of whether it is wise to fear, obey, and live as God's servants: "Teach us to count our days rightly, either as appointed for unending wrath, or for covenantal mercy, so that we might know how to pray and to live wisely." Verses 13-17 voice additional petitions that specify what such instruction would look like according to the faith that the community holds toward God. The application of this understanding, like that of Balentine, is partly a liturgical one. Christians should learn to pray in their corporate and personal worship life in the way that Psalm 90 prays.

The metaphor of translation, with its range of options from literal to dynamic equivalence to paraphrase, offers a direct yet flexible way to apply the biblical text to the contemporary context.

Contextualization as Transition/ Traduction

Transition/traduction are unfamiliar names for a familiar concept. Transition is the hermeneutical move from "then" to "now," from "what the text meant" to "what the text means." It is the model implied by the widely used metaphor of a bridge between the world of the text and the world of the reader. This model recognizes the value and the cultural authority of academic communities in establishing the historical meaning of the text and in exerting some control over how that meaning is transferred into the present. The vague term "traduction" signifies Fackre's acknowledgment that both the biblical texts and the academic context of interpretation are the products of interests that influence not only what the text means but also whom the text serves. Traduction refers to a process of identifying and negotiating the competing interests that underlie the text and the social relationships and commitments of the people who are served by the text.

The difference between transition and traduction may be a contributing factor to the traditional interpretation of Psalm 90 as a meditation on human transience. If one is looking for points of contact between the text and the contemporary context, the psalm's poetic descriptions of the brevity of human life are the most accessible starting place. Human life is short and often tragic. The psalm's reference to creation in its beginning and its generic reference to humanity in v. 3 support the interpretation of the psalm as a meditation on human existence. Critical study of the text, however, demonstrates that it is most likely the prayer of a specific community of postexilic Jews who lamented the fact not that their lives were short in relation to eternity but rather that their short lives were consumed by God's wrath without a sign of relief. The community does pray in vv. 3-6 from the perspective of their basic humanity and finitude. This theme, however, is in support of their request for relief from affliction.

The hermeneutical model of transition seeks to make connections with the psalm's description of essential human experience such as the awareness of finitude and transience. This strategy, however, says as much about the interpreters as it does about the text. A modern Enlightenment perspective projects a common human nature on all cultures and communities, and obscures the particular identities of specific communities. This tendency is evident in the history of interpretation of Psalm 90 in clear and troubling ways. Balentine has noted the broad parallel between Christian liturgical use of Psalm 90 and its treatment in Isaac Watts's famous hymn, "O God Our Help in Ages Past." Watts's hymn, written in 1714, makes use only of vv. 1-5, verses that deal with the theme of human transience in relation to divine eternality, omitting any reference to the lament of vv. 7-11 or the communal petitions of vv. 12-17. Balentine makes a connection between the hymn and Watts's stated desire to render the Psalms in such a way that he would bring "the Psalmist of Israel into the Church of Christ without anything of a Jew about him."[132] Unfortunately, the tendency to obscure the particular Jewish identity of the psalmist in favor of the most universal, and assumedly Christian, themes of the psalm was not limited to Isaac Watts alone. It has been a common trend among Christian interpreters.

The contextualizing model of traduction supplements the standard practice of hermeneutics by paying attention to the specific community reflected in the text and not only to its most universalizing human features. Such an approach to Psalm 90 asks, "Who is the community that prays this psalm? What is their situation? What communities need similar prayers for divine repentance and mercy? What is the relationship between the worshiping community and the conditions of suffering communities similar to the one given voice in Psalm 90?" This model of application of Psalm 90 brings it into continuity with the New Testament's emphasis on the church as a community of intercession.[133]

The traduction model of contextualization may find new value for Christian use of Psalm 90 in the contemporary situation of the church in North America as it recognizes and responds to the long and gradual loss of influence and status in Western culture. In an increasingly secular, post-Christian context, churches find themselves farther removed from centers of power and cultural influence than has been the case for many centuries. This new situation provides additional incentive for the church to identify with the Jewish community that prays in Psalm 90 for God's mercy and favor in the midst a long period of marginalization, rather than identifying with the perspective of all people everywhere as represented in the traditional understanding of the psalm.

Contextualization as Transformation

Many models of contextualization describe actions that readers perform on the biblical text to bring it into relationship with contemporary life. The reader is the subject and the text is the object. In the transformational model, however, the text is understood as a subject that acts and has agency in the world. This model is influenced by the theology of Karl Barth, who described the word of God as an objective reality that transforms the human experience. In the transformation model, the biblical text becomes the word of God, active and operative, an agent of change that provokes either receptive faith or active resistance.

The transformation model fits best with the results of the canonical sense of the text that interprets it from the perspective of Christian faith. Psalm 90 participates in the larger biblical story that narrates the Christian gospel in the broadest sense. As the word of God, Psalm 90 bears witness to the work of God revealed in the grand narrative of the Christian Bible.

As the prayer of the people of Israel, Psalm 90 bears witness to God's work in calling and commissioning Israel to be God's covenant people among the nations. Within this prayer, Israel confesses its faith in God as eternal Creator and Sovereign Lord. Israel also confesses God's righteousness in their communal experience of judgment. The psalm bears witness to Israel's faith in God's steadfast covenant love, both in its petitions for God to turn back to the people in mercy and also in the trust required to question unrelenting judgment. This faith provides a foundation for Israel's hope that their days of "only toil and trouble" (v. 10) may be transformed into a new time when the favor of the Lord rests upon them and the Lord establishes the works of their hands (v. 17).

A number of scholars point to the psalm's associations with Moses as an indication that it is a form of Torah instruction.[134] The psalm teaches the community to pray in a certain way, according to the pattern of Moses, who dared to ask God to repent of the wrath God planned to bring against the people and to turn toward the people in mercy and grace (Exod 32:12). Dennis Tucker provides an example of the contextualizing model of transformation in his argument that the community that prays Psalm 90 is shaped morally and theologically by the content of the psalm.[135] He identified the underlying structure of the psalm as one of exile and return. The acts of reading, praying, and internalizing the transforming language of the psalm have the power to transform the character and faith of the praying community.

James L. Mays summarized the canonical sense of Psalm 90 in a way that suggests that the structure of transformation within the psalm parallels the larger story told in the Christian Bible as a whole:

> The church reads the supplications in vv. 13-17 in light of God's revelation in Jesus Christ. He is the work of God that has decisively, once for all, changed the sign under which we live and die from wrath to grace. That is theological fact. Those in Christ use the troubles of life as chastisement and discipline. They face death in the trust that God's judgment on their sinfulness has fallen on Jesus Christ. Troubles come. Life ends. But the character of the time through which life runs to its end has been qualitatively changed. The supplications guide us to realize and be grateful for and to ask to receive what we are already been given in Jesus Christ.[136]

As Torah and gospel, the psalm instructs, shapes, and transforms its readers through worship, prayer, study, proclamation, and moral formation.

Contextualization as Trajectory

The fourth model of contextualization responds to the question of where the text is leading its readers. Texts may have implications that point beyond a position or understanding operable within the world of the text itself. Texts have implications that remain latent until events or circumstances in the cultural context activate them. Old Testament scholar John Rogerson put forward the idea that some biblical texts give witness to a new act of grace that transforms an original situation into a more redemptive situation. He termed these innovations redemption imperatives and structures of grace.[137] In such situations, it is possible not only to apply to the present context the new structure of grace described within the text but also to derive meaning from the movement within the text toward the goal of greater redemptive possibilities. In such cases, one reads and interprets not only the positions that are stated within the text but also the redemptive direction toward which the text moves. For example, the Old Testament laws that maintained the practice of indentured slavery as a form of debt payment included elements that limited the duration and effects of slavery. These limits are examples of a redemptive imperative that produced a new structure of grace. They moved the ethical status of slavery in a redemptive direction that indicated a desire to limit the practice to a temporary status. This limit moved the institution of debt slavery in the direction of freedom and equality, though admittedly by means of a long-delayed and bitterly contested process. The contextualizing model of trajectory is similar to Rogerson's concepts of the redemptive imperative and structures of grace. It looks both at the change introduced in the text and also at the direction toward which the change is moving.

What is the trajectory of Psalm 90? Where does it lead? What are the implications of the psalm? One major area of implication is for the practice of Christian corporate prayer. The psalm, like many other texts in the Old Testament, offers a candid acknowledgment of suffering and an open questioning of the idea that the duration of suffering is commensurate with the sins of the people or the covenant promises of God. In the context of American churches, the long-term, communal suffering implied in Psalm 90 has often been the experience of people of color living under the long histories of slavery, forced segregation, and continuing discrimination. When prayers of communal lament are absent from worship in privileged communities, the injustices suffered by marginalized communities can be more easily ignored or forgotten, and the complicity of privileged groups, including communities of faith, in structures of discrimination can be more easily denied.

Communal lament gives churches in privileged circumstances language to acknowledge the troubles of communities in impoverished, war-torn, and environmentally ravished regions of the world. Communal lament can connect privileged communities with the suffering of other communities beyond their own experience. "Turn, O Lord! How long? Have compassion on your servants" is a prayer that speaks directly to the urgent need of suffering people in Syria, Iraq, Somalia, Ethiopia, and Nigeria. Such prayers need to be voiced in personal and corporate worship.

Communal experiences of suffering are not limited to historically oppressed or geopolitically troubled communities, however. The economic, social, and cultural dislocations affecting American rural areas and small towns are devastating communities throughout the country. Drug and alcohol addictions, mental illness, suicide, and premature deaths have all spiked in the past two decades. The absence of practices of communal lament separates these conditions from the faith life of worshiping communities through a veil of denial. Balentine, citing numerous writings criticizing the church's neglect of the Old Testament lament tradition, argued that those criticisms have for the most part been unheeded in the church's liturgical appropriation of texts like Psalm 90.[138] This is strong evidence that interpretation of the psalm fails to appreciate the trajectory of the text that should inform the prayers of worshiping communities.

The trajectory of a text includes latent features that may be activated by changes in the church's cultural context. One major change in the American church over the last fifty years is the increasing secularization of American culture and the accelerating process of the decoupling of the church from the centers of cultural and political power in what is being labeled a post-Christian age. This cultural change brings to the forefront an issue in Psalm 90 that has mostly been neglected in Christian interpretation. The psalm speaks for a community that has suffered displacement and distress for a long time. The turning point in the psalm is a prayer for instruction and for wisdom to know how to live in a time of unrelieved distress similar to the wilderness sojourn of the exodus or the long period of exile and diaspora at the end of the Old Testament era. The psalm, as noted above, is both a prayer for Torah and a kind of Torah for a distressed and displaced community. The gift of Torah has been the sustaining spiritual resource for Judaism for millennia. Jewish communities have spent much of that time as a minority community within sometimes tolerant but often hostile majority cultures. Subtle clues within Psalm 90 point to elements of Jewish wisdom that have sustained the Jewish people as a minority religious community.

The notion of "counting our days" in v. 12 has been interpreted as a literal counting down of days during a predetermined period of affliction and as a metaphor for the finite time frame of an individual life. The psalm's reference to Moses, the wilderness period, and the language of "satisfy us in the morning" in v. 14, however, carries associations with the story of the provision of manna in the wilderness and with the institution of the Sabbath. The psalm's frequent references to periods of time and its repetition of the term "our days" (vv. 9, 12, and 14) support the idea that a daily and weekly pattern of living is central to the kind of wisdom the prayer is seeking. Counting the days of the week between Sabbaths and seeking the steadfast love of the Lord each morning like manna are important features of the Torah and wisdom of Psalm 90. Such daily and weekly patterns of worship and living are important parts of the structure of Jewish and Christian spirituality. Liturgical patterns of prayer and work have been essential in Christian monastic movements and have been a resource for Christian spirituality throughout Christian history. The changing cultural climate of a post-Christian age suggests that the daily and weekly pattern of spirituality that is latent in Psalm 90 is a prominent feature of its spiritual wisdom.

A final element of the trajectory of Psalm 90 is the degree of hope expressed within a psalm that is at the same time very honest about enduring a prolonged and agonizing experience of divine wrath. The psalm protests the experience of spending the entirety of a community's individual life spans under a period of divine wrath. Under the threat of such a reality, however, the psalm raises a faint note of hope: "Who knows?" Perhaps there is a wisdom for reckoning the community's days of affliction that only divine revelation can provide. This hope is grounded in the freedom of God to turn and show compassion and in the experience and promise of steadfast love encountered in past generations of Israel's covenant traditions.

Ancient interpreters were able to perceive the hope that lay hidden even in the starkness and darkness of the psalm's lament. Augustine argued that the attribution of the psalm to Moses was a clue that hope for salvation was already hidden within the dispensation of the Law, waiting to be revealed fully in the person of Christ. Luther wrote that even in the psalm's dark message of the wrath of God, the form of the psalm as a prayer carried within it an element of hope in the one to whom the prayer was addressed. In this way, the psalm served as an example of a hermeneutical principle that any text of the Old Testament that dealt with matters of the "first tablet," the commandments regarding worship, prayer, and holiness, carried within it a hidden witness to the resurrection.

One might object that the primary appropriations of Psalm 90 fall within a fairly limited scope of issues related to prayer and worship. In part this is due to the content and form of the psalm as a text related primarily to liturgical and theological issues. In addition, it is but one text and it cannot be expected to address matters beyond its particular concerns. On the other hand, however, it is not necessary to label concerns with prayer and worship as being limited in scope. Prayer and worship speak both to the identity of God and the identity and priorities of God's people. Prayer has the power to direct the awareness of the worshiping community toward vital needs and toward the source of life and hope. For the authors of the Psalms, prayer and worship were prominent because they represented the highest priorities of the covenant people of God.

Chapter 7

Conclusion: Worshiping God with a Wise Heart

This study grew from a quest to grasp the promise of Psalm 90: to gain the wisdom to count our days in order to make our days count. I first looked at this quest through the lens of the two most common ways of reading biblical texts like Psalm 90—religious reading and critical reading. I introduced the recent practice of theological interpretation of Scripture as an attempt to bring the strengths of these two approaches together to provide a deeper and more holistic understanding of the Bible. I specifically identified Gabriel Fackre's description of the four senses of the text as a promising model of theological interpretation, one that reads the Bible in conversation with the church, biblical scholars, theologians, and the world. I have applied this approach to Psalm 90. Now it is time to evaluate what I have learned. What does it mean to learn to count my days in order to gain a wise heart?

A comparison of examples of religious and critical readings of Psalm 90 revealed the different features of each approach. The religious approach read the psalm in light of its title as a composition of Moses. It was a prayer to be prayed by the people of the wilderness generation who were forbidden to enter the promised land as a result of their faithlessness. The critical approach traced the historical origins of the psalm to Israel's experience of exile after the fall of the final Israelite kingdom of Judah. Though the two approaches differed in methodology and interpretation, the meaning of the prayer, "teach us to count our days that we may gain a wise heart," was remarkably similar in each approach. An experience of grave punishment was the catalyst for living wisely in order to avoid further punishment in the future. In this reading, the history of Israel, whether in the wilderness period or the exile, becomes a spiritual and moral example for the reader. Israel's punishment is a lesson to ponder and apply. This understanding requires me to identify imaginatively with the experience of the Israelites in a way that motivates me to live wisely and avoid the suffering that befell them.

This interpretation of the prayer for knowledge to count our days is certainly a reasonable one, and yet it leaves something to be desired. As powerful as the motivation to avoid suffering is, there should also be a more positive reason to live wisely. The greater limitation of this interpretation, however, is that it still does not tell me how to live out the lesson of Israel's experience in specific and concrete form. If the example of Israel provides an answer to why I should count my days to gain a wise heart, it still leaves unaddressed the question of how to do this. Is it simply assumed that the reader of Psalm 90 will know how to do this?

The model of theological interpretation proposed by Fackre advises us to engage with four conversation partners in order to receive the fullest benefit from the text. The first conversation takes place among disciples within the church. The common sense of the text asks the question, "What does the text say?" from the perspective of committed members of the church body who reads it as Holy Scripture for the purposes of worship, proclamation, service, and shared communal life. Interpretation of the church's Bible begins in the church.

Reading Psalm 90 in conversation with the church widens the perspective of the psalm to take in not just Israel's history of exodus and exile but also Israel's testimony to the nature of human life as a relationship between finite creatures and their eternal creator. The statement that God turns humankind back to dust echoes the Genesis story of the first humans' expulsion from the garden in judgment for disobedience. Set within the context of the Bible's creation narrative and primeval history, the psalm's themes of the brevity of life and the experience of wrath take on a causal connection. Human life stands under judgment that renders even the longest life spans as fleeting and anxious. The prayer for knowledge to count our days is a prayer for a true understanding of the human condition. The wisdom that is most essential for proper living seems to be the wisdom that each day is precious because their number is few. The act of counting my days promises to bring wisdom because the act of counting my limited days is the very wisdom that the human condition requires.

The interpretation of the common sense of the text provides both a motivation for counting my days and a method for gaining wisdom. The wisdom that comes from recognizing the brevity of life and the value of fleeting time certainly resonates with the teaching of many religious and philosophical traditions. It is conventional wisdom that is made no easier to follow by its conventional nature. The unceasing regularity of time with its daily, seasonal, and annual rhythms habituates us into thinking that time for us will go on endlessly. The reality and inevitability of death is no less shocking in its regularity. The psalm seems to assume that we do not recognize or else choose to deny this reality and therefore need divine instruction to know how truly "to count our days." My personal experience resonates with this interpretation. The understanding of what it means to count our days that comes from conversation with the church is a helpful and necessary teaching.

The prayer for knowledge to count our days is an appropriate response to the circumstances described in Psalm 90. The prayer requests that are found in vv. 13-17, however, suggest that we need more than just the wisdom to understand that our days are limited. We also need God's mercy, which is what vv. 13-17 ask for. This series of prayers asks for a change in God, seeking a turn from wrath to mercy, from affliction to grace. Both the prayer for wisdom and the prayer for mercy seem to be appropriate and helpful, but one wonders if there is a closer connection between the two prayers than the common sense of the text reveals. The critical sense of the text answers this question in the affirmative.

The critical sense of the text comes alongside the church's common-sense reading and complements it with the gifts of wisdom that are the result of God's general revelation and the Creator's continuing blessing on humankind made in God's image. Conversation with biblical scholars sharpens the focus of the church's reading. One important clue is found in the form of the communal prayer for help that Psalm 90 shares with other prayers within the Psalter. Such prayers are not broad petitions about the human situation in general but are rather the pleas of specific communities crying out for help in situations of distress. Such prayers are uttered at the edge of a chasm between what the community knows and has come to expect about God and what they are presently experiencing in their communal life.

The community that prays in Psalm 90 knows that God "has been" the dwelling place of generations past. The community also acknowledges the common human condition of finitude and transience in relation to the eternal nature of God. In context of the communal prayer for help, however, the brevity of life is not the problem but rather is the motivation for God to help. Time is short, and the problem, as revealed in vv. 7-10, is that all of their too few days are being lived out under the circumstances of divine wrath. The people who pray in Psalm 90 do so from the midst of a great number of "days [God has] afflicted us" and the "years we have seen trouble" (v. 15).

The turning point in the psalm is the question raised in v. 11, which is a question of theodicy: "Who knows the power of your anger, and whether your wrath is greater than the fear of you?" (author's translation). The community asks whether the wrath of God that consumes all their days is more powerful than the positive benefits of their fear of God. If so, what good is it to fear God if all their days come to an end under wrath? The petition in v. 12 is essentially a request to be proven wrong. It could be paraphrased as, "Teach us how to count our days rightly so that we do not give up our proper fear of you, but rather continue to worship you with a wise heart." If the community's fears are correct that divine wrath over-whelms their faithful response, then the fear of God is not the beginning of wisdom that Prov 1:7 proclaims it to be. If, however, the community is wrong, and God is not indifferent to their devotion, then the people ask for God to correct their mistaken perception. The series of petitions in vv. 13-17 describes the form that they wish divine instruction and wisdom to take. They ask for a change in God's disposition from wrath to compassion. They ask for years of joy that are commensurate with the years of affliction they have endured. They ask that their works of service in fear of God be met not with indifference but with affirmation and significance.

The critical sense of the text demonstrates a greater sense of unity between vv. 1-12 and vv. 13-17 than what is understood in the common sense of the text or even in earlier forms of historical criticism that divided the psalm into two separate prayers between v. 12 and v. 13. The commu-nity that prays for knowledge to count their days already knows how to live. They live as servants of God (v. 13) who fear God (v. 11) and seek to worship God with a wise heart (v. 12). They simply ask for evidence in their daily experience that would affirm their faith in God's covenant loyalty.

John Goldingay has argued that attention to the grand narrative of the Bible needs to be supplemented by attention to what he calls the Bible's "middle narratives."[139] The middle narratives are intermediate stages in the biblical story that have their own internal coherence and that can function as exemplary stories for scriptural communities. In addition to the echoes of the Bible's grand narrative in Psalm 90, the critical sense of the text portrays a community at prayer against the backdrop of an implied middle narrative of long-endured affliction and diminishment. The period begin-ning with the exile and continuing through the end of the Old Testament is the middle narrative that serves as the best context for reading Psalm 90.

Critical study of the Bible is a gift from God that aids, extends, and at times even corrects the church's interpretation of Scripture. Just as theological exegesis does not begin with critical study, however, it does not end there either. The important word of critical study is not the last word. The middle narratives of the Old and New Testaments exist in the context of a broader narrative that, for Christians, is centered on the gospel of God's reconciling work in Jesus Christ. The canonical sense of the text transposes the critical sense into a new key determined by the Bible's grand narrative and its gospel focus. The recontextualization of the text in the canonical context is the product of theological reflection. It therefore calls for conversation with the church's theologians.

The canonical sense locates the text within the setting of the Old Testament canon, the New Testament canon, and the church's history of interpretation and its confessions of faith. Within the Old Testament, Psalm 90 serves as the introduction to Book IV of the Psalms. Book IV looks back to the time of God's deliverance and guidance under the leadership of Moses in the exodus and wilderness period. As such, Psalm 90 serves as a form of Torah, an instruction to the community on how to pray to God in the circumstances of communal suffering while experiencing divine hiddenness. The prayer to know how to count our days is a prayer for affirmation that obedience to Torah is a wise and faithful way to live. The tradition of the giving of manna in the wilderness, which people gathered for six days before they were provided rest on the Sabbath, is a concrete example of how to count one's days in order to come before God with a wise and faithful heart. Verse 14 asks God to "satisfy us in the morning with your steadfast love" just as God satisfied the wilderness generation each morning with the gift of manna. Torah, Sabbath observance, and a life of disciplined obedience are faithful expressions of what it means to know how to count one's days.

The New Testament context of Psalm 90 continues most of the prayer traditions portrayed in the Old Testament, including the communal prayers of lament, but adds to these a distinctly Christian practice of prayer. The model of Psalm 90 as a communal prayer is continued in New Testament instructions to pray persistently and regularly as a sign of Christian identity and as a form of spiritual discipline. The prayer of Moses is expanded by the Lord's Prayer as the community's primary model for relating to God. The language of God as eternal home is sharpened by the familial language of God as "our Father in heaven." The Christian community prays for daily bread just as the community of Psalm 90 prayed for the daily grace of being satisfied "in the morning with your steadfast love." The Lord's Prayer prays in advance for deliverance from times of trial, while Psalm 90 prays in the midst of such trials. Psalm 90's complaints about divine wrath without relief, however, are subordinated to words of commitment to God's name, God's kingdom, and God's will. Daily prayer for God's kingdom, for the essentials of bread, forgiveness, and deliverance, and for the needs of others becomes the model for how "to count our days" in the New Testament.

The impact of the life, death, and resurrection of Jesus on the church's reading of the Old Testament, including Psalm 90, is seen further in the interpretation of Christian teachers in the patristic and Reformation periods. Christian theological interpretation emphasizes the connection between Psalm 90 and the core message of the gospel about the redemption accomplished by Christ. Christian reading of the psalm follows the interplay of broad thematic elements in the psalm. Augustine and Jerome highlighted the psalm's contrast between eternal things and temporal concerns as the core message of the psalm, a message that serves as a forerunner to the ministry of Jesus. Luther highlighted evidence of the themes of law and grace in the psalm. Calvin dealt with the psalm through the lens of divine justice and mercy. Key points of contact between Psalm 90 and the ancient Christian confession preserved in the Apostle's Creed show how the essential elements of the biblical narrative guided the church in its reading of the whole Bible as a story of divine deliverance.

The canonical reading of Psalm 90 is not meant to refute or replace the critical sense of the text in its Old Testament context. Instead, it represents a recontextualization of the psalm in light of the central role of the Christ event in Christian theology as narrated in the New Testament and the wider Christian tradition. The scarcity of actual communal prayers in the New Testament and of detailed examples of worship or spiritual practice indicates that the church continued to rely on Old Testament models of spirituality in its communal and personal worship life. Though Christian interpretation focused on Jesus as the center of the biblical narrative, the Old Testament context of Psalm 90 demonstrates the way in which the Old Testament serves as both a foundation and a surplus of wisdom in addition to the essential expressions of Christian faith found in the New Testament and Christian confessions.

Study of the Bible as history or as a literary or even religious classic does not require reflection on the contemporary relevance of biblical texts. The institutional structures supporting biblical scholarship are not entirely self-perpetuating, however, and scholars do see the need to connect the results of their research to the sources of support for the institutions that fund their livelihood. On the other hand, reading the Bible as Scripture requires reflection not only on the meaning of the text but also on its significance for contemporary life and faith. The contextual sense of the text deals with the task of bridging the gap between text and world, between then and now, and between meaning and life by engaging in a conversation about the text with the world beyond the church.

In his pastoral systematics, Fackre highlighted four models of contextualization: translation, transition/traduction, transformation, and trajectory. Translation attempts to embody the meaning of the text in the life of contemporary Christians and churches in ways that honor both the givenness of the text and the realities of the contemporary context. Psalm 90 best informs contemporary faith as a model of how Christians can pray boldly and candidly in the manner of Moses as portrayed in Exodus and in the psalm itself.

The model of transition/traduction attempts to bridge the time differences between the ancient text and the contemporary culture, while remaining aware of the embedded social and political interests of the communities that produced the text and those that receive it. Psalm 90 models a practice of intercession for marginalized communities that is in continuity with the New Testament's emphasis on intercessory prayer as a spiritual discipline and a practice of ministry. This form of prayer can increase and maintain the church's awareness of its own circumstances of privilege or marginalization so that it can examine its actions and relationships appropriately.

Transformation refers to the impact that the biblical text can have on receiving communities in the form of a speech act that exerts influence and agency upon its audience. Psalm 90 points beyond itself to the narrative of God's revelation and intervention in the story of the covenant people of Israel and in the person and community of Jesus Christ. The psalm also has the potential to transform worshiping communities through its structure of lament and petition, which represents a metaphorical process of exile and return. The psalm has the power to engender a capacity for candor and hope in the communities that use it in their life of prayer.

The contextual model of trajectory asks the question of the direction in which the text moves beyond its most obvious level of meaning. What are the implications latent within the text? One implication of Psalm 90 stems from its canonical associations with the Torah. The psalm contains instruction and wisdom for navigating the continuous stream of time.

Its description of the fleeting and vexing nature of time along with the possibilities of years spent enduring affliction and trials anticipate a solution in the petitions of the concluding half of the psalm. "Counting our days" according to the fear of God holds the promise of wisdom. A daily and weekly pattern of prayer and worship as a path to wisdom in times of affliction is one of the latent messages within the psalm. This pattern of attentiveness to daily and weekly rhythms of prayer is a form of practical wisdom for navigating the challenge of living faithfully within the context of the brevity and difficulty of earthly life.

Also embedded within the structure of the psalm is a powerful endorsement of hope. Long years of affliction did not loosen the community's grip on the covenant faithfulness of God. Within in the context of the Christian canon, the psalm's affirmation of God's protection in generations past anticipated the good news of Christ that secures a hope for God's faithfulness in generations to come. Such hope is an incentive to open, persistent, intercessory prayer that is modeled in Psalm 90 and encouraged in the New Testament's instructions on prayer. The community that prays in the pattern of Psalm 90 asks for what God has already given, so that such prayers have the strongest indication of success.

Fackre's model of multiple levels of interpretation is well suited for Christian theological interpretation. It honors and respects the ability of the church to read and interpret its own Scripture. It appreciates the necessity and value of critical study of the Bible, while reserving final decisions about textual meaning and application to the believing community to whom the Bible belongs. The model allows for diverse perspectives to inform the church and to heighten the church's awareness of its own blind spots and its need for others' points of view. This variety also demonstrates how the Bible travels alongside the church through time and culture, neither calling the church back into the false hope of nostalgia nor dissolving completely into a mirror image of contemporary cultural patterns. The model avoids historical criticism's fallacy of a single, objective meaning. Yet it also helps to identify the persistent themes and range of meanings through which the text addresses the church and the world over time.

The consistent message of Psalm 90 that reverberates through each of the four senses of the text is the importance, the priority, and the fundamentally formative nature of Christian prayer as an essential centerpiece of personal faith and communal mission. The church's identity, mission, and power rest on the form, practice, and experience of personal and corporate prayer. The prayer of Moses, the man of God, prefigures and complements the prayer that Jesus taught his disciples in form, content, and persistent practice. In the language of the contextual model of transformation, Psalm 90 addresses the church with the urgent and essential nature of corporate prayer. It is both Torah and gospel. As Torah, it instructs the church in the biblical pattern of daily, weekly, fervently honest, and expectant prayer. As gospel, it points to the event in time when God most fully relented from wrath and turned toward God's people in compassion, steadfast love, splendor, and favor.

I began this study with the hope that I could find a guide for my own quest to count my days in a way that would help me to make each day count. What have I learned? I've not transformed myself into a hard-driving, hyper-programmed model of military-style efficiency; nor have I established new monastic rhythms of daily hours filled with work and prayer. I have learned a great deal from following the model of theological interpretation that seeks the common, critical, canonical, and contextual senses of the text in conversation with the church, biblical scholars, theologians, and the wider world. The obvious truth that my days are finite and numbered is one not to be ignored simply because it is obvious. I have decades of practice in denying the obvious. Psalm 90 holds me accountable to the truth about time. The teachings on Psalm 90 from Augustine, Luther, and Calvin drive this point home in vivid and compelling language.

The form of Psalm 90 as a prayer provides the second truth about my quest for making a good account of my time. Daily prayer, preferably in the morning, the time of the daily manna alluded to in v. 14 and in the daily bread of the Lord's Prayer, is a basic step in the process of learning how to count my days. The corporate form of Psalm 90 and its associations with Moses, Torah, and manna also teach me to assemble regularly, at least weekly, to observe the Christian Sabbath, the Lord's Day, and to worship with my local gathering of the covenant people, the servants of God. The phrase "that we may gain a heart of wisdom" is literally "that we may bring in a heart of wisdom." It is both a harvest image and a worship image, the results of the harvest being the substance of the sacrifice offered for the purpose of thanksgiving, communion, and reconciliation with God. The pattern of daily, weekly, and seasonal prayer through private and communal worship provides rich liturgical wisdom for counting my days and making my days count. The prayer of Psalm 90 transposed into the key of the Lord's Prayer teaches frequent, regular, persistent prayer as a mark of Christian identity and an essential spiritual discipline.

The form of Psalm 90 as a communal prayer also helps to keep my private prayer from remaining private, insular, or trivial. Psalm 90 is the prayer of a beleaguered community that has seen far too many of its finite number of days lived under wrath, when the sky seems like bronze and the face of God is hidden. I pray from within a community whose privilege often appears to protect me from many of the experiences of communities that suffer like the one represented in Psalm 90. To fail to pray specifically for communities that suffer is to ignore the New Testament's model of the church as a community of intercession and, worse, to participate tacitly if not explicitly in the unjust causes of that suffering. Certainly prayer is not enough in the face of ever-present injustice, but prayer may well be the lever that moves privileged people from the inertia of our indifference. The question of whether the wrath of God overwhelmed the faithful response of God's suffering servants is one in which I also have a stake. The faith that the fear of God remains the beginning of wisdom in the face of much evidence to the contrary gives the prayers that Psalm 90 inspires enough tension and drama to motivate even the most slothful to pray.

My study of Psalm 90 has given me clear and concrete guidance for how to improve my use of the limited time I have been given by making the finite number of my days count as a full harvest and a cheerful offering of a wise and grateful heart. Though I have learned more than even I expected from the model of theological interpretation that I have used here, I am confident that I have not come close to exhausting the rich resources of Psalm 90. In this regard, the theological interpretation of Scripture using the model outlined above is like the religious approach to reading Scripture. It finds in the Scripture a rich vein, a deep ocean, and a vast treasury of meaning. Theological interpretation provides a way to explore and enjoy these riches in conversation with the church, scholars, theologians, and the world. May these conversations continue and grow.

Notes

Chapter 1

1. Isaac Watts, 1719, "O God Our Help in Ages Past," tune ST. ANNE, lyrics available at https://hymnary.org/text/our_god_our_help_in_ages_past.

2. Kathleen Norris, *The Cloister Walk* (New York: Riverhead, 1997).

3. Rudyard Kipling, "If," in *Kipling: Poems* (Everyman's Library Pocket Poets; New York: Knopf Doubleday Publishing Group, 2013) 170.

4. W. R. L. Moberly, *Old Testament Theology: Reading the Hebrew Bible as Christian Scripture* (Grand Rapids, MI: Baker Academic, 2013) 4–5. Another example of a contribution to the topic of theological interpretation that takes the form of concrete exegesis is Stephen B. Chapman, *1 Samuel as Christian Scripture: A Theological Commentary* (Grand Rapids, MI: Eerdmans, 2015).

5. Augustine, *Confessions* 1.2, ed. and tr. Albert C. Outler, LCC (Louisville: Westminster John Knox, 2006) 32.

6. J. Richard Gott, "Our Future in the Universe," in Neil DeGrasse Tyson, Michael A. Strauss, and J. Richard Gott, *Welcome to the Universe: An Astrophysical Tour* (Princeton, NJ: Princeton University Press, 2016) 410–20.

7. For a discussion of religious and critical reading as the two primary approaches to the Bible, see Marc Zvi Brettler, Peter Enns, and Daniel J. Harrington, *The Bible and the Believer: How to Read the Bible Critically and Religiously* (New York: Oxford University Press, 2015).

8. Paul Griffiths, *Religious Reading: The Place of Reading in the Practice of Religion* (Oxford/New York: Oxford University Press, 1999) 41–43. The author's description of religious reading is helpful for understanding this approach. His comparison of religious reading to what he describes as consumerist reading seems to me to be reductionistic and polemical, however. Various nonreligious forms of reading in and beyond academic institutions have beneficial results.

9. Ibid., 46–53.

10. The historical context of the development of critical study of the Bible is described in Michael Legaspi, *The Death of Scripture and the Rise of Biblical Studies* (Oxford/New York: Oxford University Press, 2010).

11. Matthew Henry, *Exposition on the Old and New Testament*, 6 vols. (1706–1710; repr., New York: Fleming H. Revell, 1900).

12. Alan M. Harmon, "The Legacy of Matthew Henry," *Reformed Theological Review* 73 (2014): 184–87.

13. Ibid., 176–78.

14. Henry, *Exposition*, 3:870–71.

15. Jerome, "Homily 19 on Psalm 89 (90)," in *The Homilies of St. Jerome*, tr. Marie Liguoir Ewald, vol. 1, FC (Washington, D.C.: Catholic University of America Press, 1964) 146–55; Mayer I. Gruber, *Rashi's Commentary on the Psalms* (Leiden: Brill, 2004) 589–90.

16. Charles Augustus Briggs and Emilie Grace Briggs, *A Critical and Exegetical Commentary on the Book of Psalms*, vols. 1–2, ICC (New York: Charles A. Scribner's Sons, 1906–1907).

17. William L. Holladay, *The Psalms through Three Thousand Years: Prayerbook of a Cloud of Witnesses* (Minneapolis: Fortress Press, 1993) 251–52.

18. Ibid., 251.

19. Briggs, *Psalms*, 1:vii.

20. Ibid., viii.

21. Briggs, *Psalms*, 2:271–72.

22. Ibid., 274–75.

23. Jon D. Levenson, *The Hebrew Bible, the Old Testament, and Historical Criticism* (Louisville, KY: Westminster/John Knox, 1993) 123–24.

Chapter 2

24. For the argument that historical criticism devalues Scripture by locating meaning at a point in time before the text became Scripture, see Jon D. Levenson, *The Hebrew Bible*, 108–10.

25. An important resource for demonstrating the growth of biblical texts is Jeffrey Tigay, ed., *Empirical Models for Biblical Criticism* (Philadelphia: University of Pennsylvania Press, 1985). Additional evidence is discussed in Emanuel Tov, *Textual Criticism of the Hebrew Bible*, 3rd ed. (Minneapolis: Fortress, 2012) 283–324.

26. Benjamin Jowett, "On the Interpretation of Scripture," in *The Interpretation of Scripture and Other Essays* (New York: E.P. Dutton & Co., 1906) 36.

27. David Steinmetz, "The Superiority of Pre-Critical Exegesis," ThTo 37 (1980): 27–38.

28. Ibid., 38.

29. Scott W. Hahn and Benjamin Wiker, *Politicizing the Bible: The Roots of Historical Criticism and the Secularization of Scripture, 1300–1700* (New York: Crossroads, 2013).

30. Elisabeth Schüssler Fiorenza, "The Ethics of Biblical Interpretation: Decentering Biblical Scholarship," *JBL* 107 (1988): 3–17.

31. For an example of this critique from the perspective of Africa, see the comments of Musa Dube, *Postcolonial Feminist Interpretation of the Bible* (St. Louis: Chalice Press, 2000) 3.

32. James Smart, *The Strange Silence of the Bible in the Church* (Philadelphia: Westminster, 1970).

33. For an overview of recent approaches in biblical scholarship, see Steven L. McKenzie and Stephen R. Haynes, eds., *To Each Its Own Meaning: An Introduction to Biblical Criticisms and their Applications*, revised and expanded (Louisville, KY: Westminster/John Knox, 1999).

34. Michael Gorman, *Elements of Biblical Exegesis: A Basic Guide for Students and Ministers*, revised and expanded (Peabody, MA: Hendrickson, 2009).

35. These include Stephen Fowl, *Engaging Scripture: A Model for Theological Interpretation* (Oxford: Blackwell, 1998) and *Theological Interpretation of Scripture* (Eugene, OR: Cascade, 2008); Daniel J. Treier, *Introducing Theological Interpretation of Scripture* (Grand Rapids, MI: Baker Academic, 2008); J. Todd Billings, *The Word of God for the People of God: An Entryway to the Theological Interpretation of Scripture* (Grand Rapids, MI: Eerdmans, 2010); Joel B. Green, *Seized by Truth:*

Reading the Bible as Scripture (Nashville: Abingdon, 2007) and *Practicing Theological Interpretation: Engaging Biblical Texts for Faith and Formation* (Grand Rapids, MI: Baker Academic, 2012).

36. Kevin J. Vanhoozer, ed. *Dictionary for Theological Interpretation of the Bible* (Grand Rapids, MI: Baker Academic, 2005).

37. Gorman, *Elements*, 146.

38. Fowl, *Theological Interpretation*, 6–8.

39. Fowl, *Engaging Scripture*, 2–3.

40. Green, *Seized By Truth*, 11–12. On the virtues expected of the implied reader of the Bible, see Richard S. Briggs, *The Virtuous Reader: Old Testament Narrative and Interpretive Virtue*, Studies in Theological Interpretation (Grand Rapids, MI: Baker Academic, 2010). On theological interpretation as a hermeneutic of trust, see Gorman, *Elements*, 142–43.

41. In his introduction to theological interpretation, Daniel Treier identifies the recovery of ancient practices of Scripture interpretation as a major catalyst of the movement. See *Introducing Theological Interpretation*, 39–55.

42. For a discussion of the role of saintly interpreters in theological interpretation, see L. Gregory Jones, "Embodying Scripture in the Community of Faith," in Ellen F. Davis and Richard B. Hays, eds., *The Art of Reading Scripture* (Grand Rapids, MI: Eerdmans, 2003) 147–54.

43. Gabriel Fackre, "Bible, Community, and Spirit," *HBT* 21 (1999): 76.

44. Brevard S. Childs, *Introduction to the Old Testament as Scripture* (Philadelphia: Fortress, 1979), and *Biblical Theology of the Old and New Testaments: Theological Reflection on the Christian Bible* (Minneapolis: Fortress, 1992).

45. Childs, *Exodus: A Commentary*, OTL (Philadelphia: Westminster, 1974).

46. Gabriel Fackre, *Authority: Scripture in the Church for the World*, vol. 2 in *The Christian Story: A Pastoral Systematics* (Grand Rapids, MI: William B. Eerdmans, 1987). A summary and example of his model is found in "Bible, Community, Spirit."

47. Fackre, *Authority*, 163–64.

48. Fackre, "Bible, Community, Spirit," 76–78.

49. Fackre, *Authority*, 176–78.

50. Ibid., 212, 243–51.

Chapter 3
51. Ibid.

52. This history is summarized in a helpful way in R. W. L. Moberly, *The Bible in a Disenchanted Age: The Enduring Possibility of Christian Faith* (Grand Rapids, MI: Baker Academic, 2018) 19–23.

53. Gorman, *Elements*.

54. For a discussion of these terms, see Gordon D. Fee and Mark L. Strauss, *How to Choose a Translation for All It's Worth* (Grand Rapids, MI: Zondervan, 2007) 26–28.

55. Augustine, *Exposition on the Book of Psalms*, vol. 8 in NPNF[1], ed. Philip Schaff (Peabody, MA: Hendrickson, 1994) 441–46.

56. I follow the practice of most printed English Bibles in using the term "Lord" in regular type to indicate the Hebrew title "Lord," and using the term LORD in small uppercase letters to indicate the Hebrew name Yahweh. The Hebrew name Yahweh only occurs in v. 13 of Psalm 90.

57. James L. Mays, *Psalms*, Interpretation Commentary (Louisville, KY: Westminster/John Knox, 1994) 295.

Chapter 4
58. Fackre, *Authority*, 168.

59. Ibid., 176.

60. John H. Hayes and Carl R. Holladay, *Biblical Exegesis: A Beginner's Handbook*, 3rd ed. (Louisville, KY: Westminster/John Knox, 2007). For a similar introduction, see McKenzie and Haynes, *To Each Its Own Meaning*.

61. For example, H. J. Kraus, *Theology of the Psalms*, tr. Keith D. Crim (Philadelphia: Augsburg, 1970) 334.

62. Franz Delitzsch, *Biblical Commentary on the Psalms*, tr. David Eaton, vol. 3 (London: Hodder & Stoughton, 1889) 2–17.

63. Marvin J. Tate, *Psalms 51–100*, WBC 20B (Dallas: Word, 1994) 437–38.

64. Gerard H. Wilson, *The Editing of the Hebrew Psalter*, SBLDS 76 (Chico, CA: Scholars, 1985) 187.

65. Ibid., 215.

66. Susan Gillingham, "Psalms 90–106: Book Four and the Covenant with David," *European Judaism* 48 (2015): 88.

67. Tate, *Psalms 51–100*, 439.

68. Gerhard von Rad, *God at Work in Israel*, tr. John H. Marks (Nashville: Abingdon, 1980) 210–23.

69. Tate, *Psalms 51–100*, 439.

70. Eberhard Gerstenberger, *Psalms, Part 2, and Lamentations*, FOTL XV (Grand Rapids, MI: Eerdmans, 2001) 161–62.

71. Richard J. Clifford, "What Does the Psalmist Ask for in Psalms 39:5 and 90:12?" *JBL* 119 (2000): 59-66; and "Psalm 90: Wisdom Meditation or Communal Lament?" in *The Book of Psalms: Composition and Reception*, ed. P. Flint and P. Miller, VT Supp 99 (Leiden: Brill, 2005) 190–205.

72. J. J. M. Roberts, "Of Signs, Prophets, and Time Limits: A Note on Psalm 74:9," *CBQ* 39 (1977): 474–81.

73. Samuel Balentine, "Turn, O Lord! How Long?" *R&E* 100/3 (2003): 468.

74. Frank-Lothar Hossfeld and Eric Zenger, *Psalms 2: A Commentary on Psalms 51–100*, ed. Klaus Baltzer (Minneapolis: Fortress, 2005) 419.

75. Ibid.

76. Ibid.

77. Tate, *Psalms 51–100*, 437.

78. For a different conclusion about v. 16, see Hossfeld and Zenger, *Psalms 2*, 419–20. They connect v. 16 with vv. 13-15.

79. W. Dennis Tucker Jr., "*Exitus, Reditus*, and Moral Formation in Psalm 90," in *Diachronic and Synchronic: Reading the Psalms in Real Time*, ed. J. S. Burnett, W. H. Bellinger, Jr., and W. Dennis Tucker, Jr., LHBOT 488 (New York: T & T Clark, 2007) 152.

80. Tucker argues that the perfect form of the verb in v. 1 indicates that the statement about God as a dwelling place is describing a past reality ("*Exitus*," 151).

81. See the discussion in Tate, *Psalms 51–100*, 439, and in Gerstenberger, *Psalms*, 161–62.

82. Tucker, "*Exitus*,"152.

83. The translation of Psalm 90 in the detailed analysis section of this chapter is the author's translation.

84. David Noel Freedman, "Who Asks (or Tells) God to Repent?" *Bible Review* 1 (1985): 56–59. See also Balentine, "Turn, O Lord," 469–75.

85. Mays, *Psalms*, 291.

86. Clifford, "What Does the Psalmist Ask," 197; Tucker, "*Exitus*," 148, n. 22.

87. Clifford, "What Does the Psalmist Ask," 65.

88. Ibid., 64, n. 17.

89. Tov, *Textual Criticism,* 221, 332.

90. Bruce K. Waltke and M. O'Connor, *An Introduction to Biblical Hebrew Syntax* (Winona Lake, WI: Eisenbrauns, 1990) 265.

Chapter 5

91. The theological nature of the formation of the canon is described in Brevard S. Childs, *Biblical Theology,* 70–72.

92. For a discussion of the theological reasons for maintaining the separate integrity of the Old Testament apart from but also in dialogue with Christian theology, see Chapman, *1 Samuel as Christian Scripture*, 5–10.

93. Robert W. Jenson, *Canon and Creed* (Louisville, KY: Westminster John Knox Press, 2010) 14.

94. Tate, *Psalms 51–100,* 530.

95. Balentine, "'Turn, O Lord!," 465–75. See also J. Clinton McCann, "Psalms," in *New Interpreter's Bible*, ed. Leader Keck et al., vol. 4 (Nashville: Abingdon, 1996) 1040.

96. In addition to Deut 6:13, see also 4:10; 5:29; 6:2, 24; 8:6; 10:12, 20; 13:4; 14:23; 17:19; 28:58; and 31:12.

97. McCann, "Psalms," 1040–42.

98. Patrick Miller, *They Cried to the Lord: The Form and Theology of Biblical Prayer* (Minneapolis: Fortress, 1994) 304–307.

99. Dietrich Bonhoeffer, *Life Together and Psalms: The Prayer Book of the Bible* (Minneapolis: Augsburg, 1996) 177.

100. Miller, *They Cried*, 311–12.

101. Pss 25:11; 31:3; 79:9; 109:21; and 143:11.

102. Miller, *They Cried*, 321–24.

103. Ibid., 325–26.

104. A helpful description of the sophisticated methods of patristic interpretation is found in John J. O'Keefe and R. R. Reno, *Sanctified Vision: An Introduction to Early Christian Interpretation of the Bible* (Baltimore: Johns Hopkins Press, 2005) 24–68.

105. Quentin Wesselschmidt, ed., "Psalms 51–150," vol. 8 of *Ancient Christian Commentary on Scripture: Old Testament* (Downer's Grove, IL: InterVarsity Press, 2007) 169.

106. Augustine, *Exposition*, 441.

107. Ibid., 445–46.

108. Jerome, "Homily 19 on Psalm 89 (90)," 146–55.

109. Gregory of Nyssa, *Commentary on the Inscriptions of the Psalms*, tr. Casimir McCambley (Brookline, MA: Hellenic College Press, 1990) 40–41.

110. Martin Luther, *Selected Psalms*, vol. 13 in Luther's Works, American edition (55 vols.), ed. Jaroslav Pelikan and tr. Paul Bretscher (St. Louis: Concordia Publishing House, 1956) 75–142.

111. Ibid., 76–77.

112. Ibid., 100.

113. Ibid., 129–30.

114. Ibid., 131–41.

115. Ibid., 110–12.

116. John Calvin, *Commentary on the Book of Psalms*, tr. James Anderson, vol. 3 (Edinburgh: Calvin Translation Society, 1845), available at <https://www.ccel. org/ccel/calvin/calcom10.xxv.html>.

117. Fackre, *Authority*, 178.

118. Ibid., 182.

119. Wesselschmidt, "Psalm 51–150," 167.

120. Augustine, *Exposition*, 444; Jerome, "Homily," 153.

121. Fredrick C. Holmgren, *The Old Testament and the Significance of Jesus* (Grand Rapids, MI: Wm B Eerdmans, 1999) 107.

Chapter 6
122. Fackre, *Authority*, 212.

123. Ibid.

124. For a discussion of the role of hermeneutic theory in theological interpretation, see Treier, *Introducing Theological Interpretation*, 127–56. For an argument that theological interpretation does not necessarily require a general theory of hermeneutics, see Fowl, *Theological Interpretation of Scripture*, 38–48, and also Kevin J. Vanhoozer, "Introduction: What Is Theological Interpretation of the Bible?" in K. Vanhoozer, ed., *Dictionary for Theological Interpretation of the Bible* (Grand Rapids, MI: Baker Academic, 2005) 19.

125. Fackre, *Authority*, 243–45.

126. The Consultation on Common Texts, *The Revised Common Lectionary* (Nashville: Abingdon, 1992) 38.

127. Mays, *Psalms*, 292. See the similar description of Artur Weiser, *The Psalms: A Commentary*, tr. Herbert Hartwell (OTL; Philadelphia: Westminster, 1962) 598–99; and Terence Fretheim, "Theological Reflections on the Wrath of God in the Old Testament, *HBT* 24 (2002): 1–26.

128. Luther, *Selected Psalms*, 130.

129. Weiser, *The Psalms*, 601.

130. Clifford, "What Does the Psalmist Ask?," 62–66.

131. Balentine, "Turn, O Lord!," 467.

132. Ibid., 475.

133. Miller, *They Cried*, 325–27.

134. Mays, *Psalms*, 294; Balentine, "Turn, O Lord," 467; McCann, "Psalms," 1040–43.

135. Tucker, "*Exitus*," 146–52.

136. Mays, *Psalms*, 295.

137. John Rogerson, *Theory and Practice in Old Testament Ethics*, ed. M. Daniel Carroll, JSOTSup 405 (London: T&T Clark, 2004) 24–28.

138. Balentine, "Turn, O Lord," 274–75.

Conclusion
139. John Goldingay, *Do We Need the New Testament? Letting the Old Testament Speak for Itself* (Downer's Grove, IL: InterVarsity Press, 2015) 69–90.

Bibliography

Augustine. *Confessions*. Edited and translated by Albert C. Outler. LCC. Louisville: Westminster John Knox, 2006.

———. *Exposition on the Book of Psalms*. In vol. 8 of *The Nicene and Post-Nicene Fathers*, Series 1. Edited by Philip Schaff. 1886–1889. 14 vols. Repr., Peabody, MA: Hendrickson, 1994.

Balentine, Samuel. "Turn, O Lord! How Long?" *R&E* 100/3 (2003): 465–81.

Billings, J. Todd. *The Word of God for the People of God: An Entryway to the Theological Interpretation of Scripture*. Grand Rapids, MI: Eerdmans, 2010.

Bonhoeffer, Dietrich. *Life Together and Psalms: The Prayer Book of the Bible*. Minneapolis: Augsburg, 1996.

Brettler, Marc Zvi, Peter Enns, and Daniel J. Harrington. *The Bible and the Believer: How to Read the Bible Critically and Religiously*. New York: Oxford University Press, 2015.

Briggs, Charles Augustus, and Emilie Grace Briggs. *A Critical and Exegetical Commentary on the Book of Psalms*. 2 vols. ICC. New York: Charles A. Scribner's Sons, 1906–1907.

Briggs, Richard S. *The Virtuous Reader: Old Testament Narrative and Interpretive Virtue*, Studies in Theological Interpretation. Grand Rapids, MI: Baker Academic, 2010.

Calvin, John. *Commentary on the Book of Psalms*. Translated by James Anderson. Vol. 3. Edinburgh: Calvin Translation Society, 1845. Available at <https://www.ccel.org/ccel/calvin/calcom10.xxv.html>.

Chapman, Stephen B. *1 Samuel as Christian Scripture: A Theological Commentary*. Grand Rapids, MI: Eerdmans, 2015.

Childs, Brevard S. *Biblical Theology of the Old and New Testaments: Theological Reflection on the Christian Bible.* Minneapolis: Fortress, 1992.

———. *Introduction to the Old Testament as Scripture.* Philadelphia: Fortress, 1979.

———. *Exodus: A Commentary.* OTL. Philadelphia: Westminster, 1974.

Clifford, Richard J. "Psalm 90: Wisdom Meditation or Communal Lament?" Pages 190–205 in *The Book of Psalms: Composition and Reception.* Edited by Peter W. Flint and Patrick Miller. VT Supp 99. Leiden: Brill, 2005.

———. "What Does the Psalmist Ask for in Psalms 39:5 and 90:12?" *JBL* 119 (2000): 59–66.

The Consultation on Common Texts. *The Revised Common Lectionary.* Nashville: Abingdon, 1992.

Davis, Ellen F., and Richard B. Hays, eds. *The Art of Reading Scripture.* Grand Rapids, MI: Eerdmans, 2003.

Delitzsch, Franz. *Biblical Commentary on the Psalms.* Translated by David Eaton. Vol. 3. London: Hodder & Stoughton, 1889.

Dube, Musa. *Postcolonial Feminist Interpretation of the Bible.* St. Louis: Chalice Press, 2000.

Fackre, Gabriel. *Authority: Scripture in the Church for the World.* Vol. 2 in *The Christian Story: A Pastoral Systematics.* Grand Rapids, MI: William B. Eerdmans, 1987.

———. "Bible, Community, and Spirit." *HBT* 21 (1999): 66–81.

Fee, Gordon D., and Mark L. Strauss. *How to Choose a Translation for All That Its Worth.* Grand Rapids, MI: Zondervan, 2007.

Fowl, Stephen. *Engaging Scripture: A Model for Theological Interpretation.* Oxford: Blackwell, 1998.

———. *Theological Interpretation of Scripture.* Eugene, OR: Cascade, 2008.

Freedman, David Noel. "Who Asks (or Tells) God to Repent?" *Bible Review* 1 (1985): 56–59.

Fretheim, Terence. "Theological Reflections on the Wrath of God in the Old Testament." *HBT* 24 (2002): 1–26.

Gerstenberger, Eberhard. *Psalms, Part 2, and Lamentations.* FOTL XV. Grand Rapids, MI: Eerdmans, 2001.

Gillingham, Susan. "Psalms 90–106: Book Four and the Covenant with David." *European Judaism* 48 (2015): 83–101.

Goldingay, John. *Do We Need the New Testament? Letting the Old Testament Speak for Itself.* Downer's Grove, IL: InterVarsity Press, 2015.

Gorman, Michael J. *Elements of Biblical Exegesis: A Basic Guide for Students and Ministers.* Revised and expanded. Peabody, MA: Hendrickson, 2009.

Gott, J. Richard. "Our Future in the Universe," Pages 400–24 in Neil DeGrasse Tyson, Michael A. Strauss, and J. Richard Gott. *Welcome to the Universe: An Astrophysical Tour.* Princeton, NJ: Princeton University Press, 2016.

Green, Joel B. *Practicing Theological Interpretation: Engaging Biblical Texts for Faith and Formation.* Grand Rapids, MI: Baker Academic, 2012.

———. *Seized by Truth: Reading the Bible as Scripture.* Nashville: Abingdon, 2007.

Gregory of Nyssa. *Commentary on the Inscriptions of the Psalms.* Translated by Casimir McCambley. Brookline, MA: Hellenic College Press, 1990.

Griffiths, Paul. *Religious Reading: The Place of Reading in the Practice of Religion.* Oxford/New York: Oxford University Press, 1999.

Gruber, Mayer I. *Rashi's Commentary on the Psalms.* Leiden: Brill, 2004.

Harmon, Alan M. "The Legacy of Matthew Henry." *Reformed Theological Review* 73 (2014): 181–97.

Hahn, Scott W., and Benjamin Wiker. *Politicizing the Bible: The Roots of Historical Criticism and the Secularization of Scripture, 1300–1700.* New York: Crossroads, 2013.

Hayes, John H., and Carl R. Holladay. *Biblical Exegesis: A Beginner's Handbook.* 3rd ed. Louisville, KY: Westminster/John Knox, 2007.

Henry, Matthew. *Exposition on the Old and New Testament.* 6 vols. 1706–1710. Repr., New York: Fleming H. Revell, 1900.

Holladay, William L. *The Psalms through Three Thousand Years: Prayerbook of a Cloud of Witnesses.* Minneapolis: Fortress Press, 1993.

Holmgren, Fredrick C. *The Old Testament and the Significance of Jesus.* Grand Rapids, MI: Wm B Eerdmans, 1999.

Hossfeld, Frank-Lothar and Eric Zenger. *Psalms 2: A Commentary on Psalms 51–100.* Edited by Klaus Baltzer. Translated by Linda M. Mahony. Hermeneia. Minneapolis: Fortress, 2005.

Jenson, Robert W. *Canon and Creed.* Louisville, KY: Westminster John Knox Press, 2010.

Jerome. "Homily 19 on Psalm 89 (90)." Pages 146–55 in *The Homilies of St. Jerome.* Translated by Marie Liguori Ewald. Vol. 1. FC. Washington, DC: Catholic University of America Press, 1964.

Jones, L. Gregory. "Embodying Scripture in the Community of Faith." Pages 147–54 in Ellen F. Davis and Richard B. Hays, eds. *The Art of Reading Scripture.* Grand Rapids, MI: Eerdmans, 2003.

Jowett, Benjamin. "On the Interpretation of Scripture." Pages 1–76 in *The Interpretation of Scripture and Other Essays.* New York: E.P. Dutton & Co., 1906.

Kraus, H. J. *Theology of the Psalms.* Translated by Keith R. Crim. Philadelphia: Augsburg, 1979.

Legaspi, Michael. *The Death of Scripture and the Rise of Biblical Studies.* Oxford/ New York: Oxford University Press, 2010.

Levenson, Jon D. *The Hebrew Bible, the Old Testament, and Historical Criticism.* Louisville, KY: Westminster/John Knox, 1993.

Luther, Martin. "Lecture on Psalm 90, 1534." Translated by Paul M. Bretscher. Pages 75–141 in vol. 13 of *Luther's Works.* American Edition, 55 vols. Edited by Jaroslav Pelikan and Helmut T. Lehman. Philadephia: Muehlenberg and Fortress, and St. Louis: Concordia, 1955–86.

Mays, James L. *Psalms,* Interpretation Commentary. Louisville, KY: Westminster/ John Knox, 1994.

McCann, J. Clinton. "Psalms." Pages 639–1279 in *New Interpreter's Bible.* Edited by Leader Keck et al. Vol. 4. Nashville: Abingdon, 1996.

McKenzie, Steven L. and Stephen R. Haynes, eds. *To Each Its Own Meaning: An Introduction to Biblical Criticisms and their Applications*, revised and expanded. Louisville, KY: Westminster/John Knox, 1999.

Miller, Patrick. *They Cried to the Lord: The Form and Theology of Biblical Prayer.* Minneapolis: Fortress, 1994.

Moberly, R. W. L. *The Bible in a Disenchanted Age: The Enduring Possibility of Christian Faith.* Grand Rapids, MI: Baker Academic, 2018.

———. *Old Testament Theology: Reading the Hebrew Bible as Christian Scripture.* Grand Rapids, MI: Baker Academic, 2013.

Norris, Kathleen. *The Cloister Walk.* New York: Riverhead, 1997.

O'Keefe, John J., and R. R. Reno. *Sanctified Vision: An Introduction to Early Christian Interpretation of the Bible.* Baltimore: Johns Hopkins Press, 2005.

Rad, Gerhard von. *God at Work in Israel.* Translated by John H. Marks. Nashville: Abingdon, 1980.

Roberts, J. J. M. "Of Signs, Prophets, and Time Limits: A Note on Psalm 74:9." *CBQ* 39 (1977): 474–81.

Rogerson, John. *Theory and Practice in Old Testament Ethics.* Edited by M. Daniel Carroll R. JSOTSup 405. London: T&T Clark, 2004.

Schüssler Fiorenza, Elisabeth. "The Ethics of Biblical Interpretation: Decentering Biblical Scholarship." *JBL* 107 (1988): 3–17.

Smart, James D. *The Strange Silence of the Bible in the Church.* Philadelphia: Westminster, 1970.

Steinmetz, David. "The Superiority of Pre-Critical Exegesis." *ThTo* 37 (1980): 27–38.

Tate, Marvin J. *Psalms 51–100.* WBC 20B. Dallas, TX: Word, 1990.

Tigay, Jeffrey, ed. *Empirical Models for Biblical Criticism.* Philadelphia: University of Pennsylvania Press, 1985.

Tov, Emanuel. *Textual Criticism of the Hebrew Bible.* 3rd ed. Minneapolis: Fortress, 2012.

Treier, Daniel J. *Introducing Theological Interpretation of Scripture*. Grand Rapids, MI: Baker Academic, 2008.

Tucker, W. Dennis, Jr. "*Exitus, Reditus*, and Moral Formation in Psalm 90." Pages 143–54 in *Diachronic and Synchronic: Reading the Psalms in Real Time*. Edited by J. S. Burnett, W. H. Bellinger Jr., and W. Dennis Tucker Jr. LHBOT 488. New York: T & T Clark, 2007.

Vanhoozer, Kevin J. "Introduction: What Is Theological Interpretation of the Bible?" Pages 19–25 in K. Vanhoozer, ed. *Dictionary for Theological Interpretation of the Bible*. Grand Rapids, MI: Baker Academic, 2005.

Waltke, Bruce K., and M. O'Connor. *An Introduction to Biblical Hebrew Syntax*. Winona Lake, WI: Eisenbrauns, 1990.

Weiser, Artur. *The Psalms: A Commentary*. Translated by Herbert Hartwell. OTL. Philadelphia: Westminster, 1962.

Wesselschmidt, Quentin F., ed. "Psalms 51–150." Vol. 8 of *Ancient Christian Commentary on Scripture: Old Testament*. Downer's Grove, IL: InterVarsity Press, 2007.

Wilson, Gerard H. *The Editing of the Hebrew Psalter*. SBLDS 76. Chico, CA: Scholars, 1985.

www.ingramcontent.com/pod-product-compliance
Lightning Source LLC
Chambersburg PA
CBHW071346090426
42738CB00012B/3033